The Science of Foreknowledge

Being a Compendium of Astrological Research, Philosophy, & Practice in the East & West; Containing Material Now Otherwise Inaccessible to the Student, & the Radix System or Method of Directing for Future Events & Tendencies as Used by the Author & Hitherto Unpublished. Partial Contents: Astrology in Shakespeare; The Great Year; Celestial Dynamics; Neptune; New Satellite Lilith; A Third Earth-Moon; Indian Astrology; Horoscope of Rama; Astrology of the Hebrews; Star of Bethlehem; Measure of life; Astrological Practice, Ptolemys' method, Bonatti's method of direction; Radix System; Our solar system.

Sepharial

ISBN 1-56459-717-2

Kessinger Publishing's
Rare Mystical Reprints

THOUSANDS OF SCARCE BOOKS
ON THESE AND OTHER SUBJECTS:

Freemasonry * Akashic * Alchemy * Alternative Health * Ancient Civilizations * Anthroposophy * Astrology * Astronomy * Aura * Bible Study * Cabalah * Cartomancy * Chakras * Clairvoyance * Comparative Religions * Divination * Druids * Eastern Thought * Egyptology * Esoterism * Essenes * Etheric * ESP * Gnosticism * Great White Brotherhood * Hermetics * Kabalah * Karma * Knights Templar * Kundalini * Magic * Meditation * Mediumship * Mesmerism * Metaphysics * Mithraism * Mystery Schools * Mysticism * Mythology * Numerology * Occultism * Palmistry * Pantheism * Parapsychology * Philosophy * Prosperity * Psychokinesis * Psychology * Pyramids * Qabalah * Reincarnation * Rosicrucian * Sacred Geometry * Secret Rituals * Secret Societies * Spiritism * Symbolism * Tarot * Telepathy * Theosophy * Transcendentalism * Upanishads * Vedanta * Wisdom * Yoga * Plus Much More!

DOWNLOAD A FREE CATALOG AT:
www.kessinger.net

OR EMAIL US AT:
books@kessinger.net

INTRODUCTION

The following pages are intended to bring some of the more recondite and controversial aspects of the Science of Foreknowledge into discussion; and, further, to supply a great deal of abstruse information not otherwsie accessible to the student. That there are problems yet before the student of Astrology, and matters which cannot be determined out of hand save by a direct appeal to the facts of experience, should serve to prove that the subject treated of is not immersed in that haze of superstition to which irresponsible writers, ignorant alike of the principles and teachings of Astrology, have been wont to consign it. It is hoped that the large variety of subjects dealt with in the course of this work will not obscure the main object to which it is directed—namely, the affirmation from experience of a veritable Science of Cosmical Interpretation, as fully deserving of study and recognition as is the science of astronomy from which it springs. For the rest, I am content to leave my work in the hands of those who are qualified to appreciate and to criticize it.

SEPHARIAL.

London, 1918.

CONTENTS

	PAGE
INTRODUCTION	v
THE SCIENCE OF FOREKNOWLEDGE	1
R. A. PROCTOR ON ASTROLOGY	8
ASTROLOGY IN SHAKESPEARE	15
THE GREAT YEAR	22
CELESTIAL DYNAMICS	29
NEPTUNE	34
THE NEW SATELLITE LILITH	39
A THIRD EARTH-MOON	46
THE ASTROLOGY OF LILITH	50
INDIAN ASTROLOGY	58
THE EVIDENCE OF AUTHORITY	71
HOROSCOPE OF RAMA	81
THE ASTROLOGY OF THE HEBREWS	88
THE STAR OF BETHLEHEM	104
JOAN OF ARC	111
THE MEASURE OF LIFE	118
ASTROLOGICAL PRACTICE:	
PTOLEMYS' METHOD	126
BONATTI'S METHOD OF DIRECTING	129
THE RADIX SYSTEM	132
HOROSCOPICAL ANOMALIES	141
STUDIES IN BRIEF	145
OUR SOLAR SYSTEM	148
FINANCIAL ASTROLOGY	152
APPENDIX	159

THE SCIENCE OF FOREKNOWLEDGE

THE statement of Professor Sir Oliver Lodge, made before the British Association (Mathematical Section) at Bristol some years ago—viz., "If once we grasp the idea that the *past* and *future* may be *actually existing*, we can recognize that they may have a controlling influence upon all present action"—is one worthy of considering in its fullest significance. That the *past* exerts a "controlling influence" on all present action is so clear as to have been commonly received into our system of thought as a truism. It asserts the obvious, that the effect follows, and is dependent upon, its cause. But that the unrevealed future should have a controlling influence of a similar nature upon the thought, feeling, and volition of the moment is a novel and daring argument to voice in the presence of a scientific body. For what is it in essence but a statement of pre-established harmony, fore-ordination, and the inevitable, as controlling the present towards a "definite and preconceived end" by the process of an orderly unfoldment? It postulates man as the subject of a certain destiny, and human endeavour as the fulfilling of Fate. Not only is there the *past* exerted along the lines of racial evolution, national growth, and heredity, but also a very definite and constant *pull* in the direction to which that evolution is impelled by the Divine Will as expressed in the operations of natural law.

The position taken up by the great scientist is of immense significance to the student of astrology, inasmuch as it defines the scientific attitude in regard to the common ground of astrological doctrine and practice, which conceives the future of an individual or a race to be foreshadowed in the horoscopical conditions of its genesis, and therefore perpetually operative from the first moment of existence to the production of such predetermined ends.

From the belief that the future exerts an influence on present action to the belief that the future (as *actually existing* with the past and present) may be capable of direct study and cognition is a step already taken by every student of astrology, and one that is even essayed—though somewhat timidly—by more than one accredited exponent of scientific thought. The day will come, as surely as the rising of the sun, when "the controlling influence" of planetary action on human destiny will be recognized equally with the solidarity of the solar system or the attraction of gravitation.

Sir Oliver Lodge is not alone in this conviction of the significance of an impinging futurity, as shown by the following contribution to the subject by the Rev. Maurice Davies, the well-known author of "Orthodox London." It is in itself a refutation of the common prejudice against astrology in the minds of those who are wholly ignorant of its principles, its practice, its teachings, and its place in the scheme of educated thought. He writes:

"Among all the various forms of occultation, surely this is the one to which that self-stultifying word 'supernatural' is least applicable. If the Sun and Moon sway the tides, why should they leave man untouched? If the testimony of language be worth anything, Greek, Latin, and English bear evidence that the 'moonstruck' owe their infirmity to the evil influence of our satellite. But it is not my present purpose to argue about theories, or refer to other

"What I have to do is to give such passages of my own personal history as appear to establish the fact that 'the stars in their courses' do affect our destinies, and that it is possible for gifted persons to read those destinies, not only as fulfilled in the past, but as lying stored up for us in the future. I shall be inartistic enough, then, to give an instance of this in my own experience, which is quite as remarkable as any of which I have ever read in tale or history. Of course, according to artistic rules, this episode ought to be reserved as a *bonne-bouche* until the last, but I give it here at the outset, if only to guard against the supposition of being 'moonstruck' myself. I can see no explanation of the facts short of believing that astrology is just as much a fixed science as astronomy.

"Fortunately I am able in this instance to give names in full, so that my narrative may be checked if necessary. The astrologer who figures in this case is Mr. T. L. Henly, a gentleman who has made it his mission in life to develop the cultivation of flax as a home industry, and who has taken out several patents for that fibre. But, like the Swedish seer Swedenborg, Mr. Henly combines with his practical and material pursuit a strong taste for occultism. He is, at the time I write (November, 1896), living and working successfully, so that he can 'witness if I lie.'

"He had been dining with me one Sunday, and went to sit 'under me' in the evening at a parish church in the suburbs, where I was Sunday evening lecturer. As we were walking to church he said, 'I have been looking over your horoscope, and I find there is a windfall coming to you in a month's time.'

"I told him I was extremely glad to hear it, and naturally inquired whether he could inform me how this particular windfall was to come. 'Yes,' he said, 'it would be occasioned by a death.' I cast about, and said there was only one person in existence whose death would be likely to benefit me. Could he be alluding to the unexpected death of this old lady?

No, it was not a lady. It was a gentleman, whose death would do me good. The death, he said, would be the result of an accident. 'And, moreover,' he added, ' it is a death which will be talked of from one end of England to the other.'

"I quite failed to guess who my illustrious friend or relative could be, and concluded in my omniscience that he was talking at random. We changed the subject. I preached my sermon, and soon forgot all about the prognostication. A month from the date on which this prophecy had been uttered was Whit-Sunday. I was still combining journalistic work with my clerical and scholastic duties, and just then I used to write four leaders each week for Mr. Edward Spender, who was editor of the National Press Agency in Shoe Lane, and also London editor and part proprietor of the *Western Morning News*. Every now and then Mr. Spender used to go to Plymouth for the purpose of auditing the accounts of his journal, and on those occasions I had to fill his chair at the National Press Agency.

"On the day succeeding the Whit-Sunday I went down to the office, as Mr. Spender was then absent on one of his expeditions to the West of England, when I found on my desk a telegram containing the following words: '*Mr. Spender and his two sons were drowned yesterday at Plymouth*.' Then I remembered the prophecy of a month back, and felt how false the prediction was. Instead of being a windfall, this event had put a sudden stop to work which had been pleasant, and in my modest estimation fairly remunerative.

"It was quite true that the death was talked of from one end of England to the other. It was, in journalistic language, 'startling.' The father and two sons were bathing in Whitsand Bay, when a tidal wave came and swept them off. The event is commemorated in a monument which stands on the shores of the bay.

"But a windfall to me! How could that be? Well, it was so, after all, for, quite contrary to my expectation, I succeeded to Mr. Spender's editorship, and retained it for several years, until I vacated it for another appointment.

"The prophecy, therefore, was correct in every detail, and, as I have said, it was given to me a full month before its fulfilment exactly as I have here reported it. I am quite at a loss to guess what 'explanation' could be given of these facts, save that the coming event had cast its shadow before, and that Mr. Henly read that event in my horoscope as in a book. I need scarcely add, since it will have been apparent on the face of my narrative, that there was no 'professional' in all this. Not only did Mr. Henly give his prophecy without fee or reward, but he also added such instructions to my wife as to enable her to develop her gift, and I am thus fortunate in possessing a Sibylline oracle under my own roof.

* * * * *

"Surely the case I have cited might go some way towards answering the question as to the *cui bono* of occultism. As I am not ambitious of writing a folio, I must content myself with these examples of astrology proper, which, it will be seen, are happily free from that vagueness which too often accompanies oracular responses. In fact, I must in justice say that I have never met in this branch of the occult with anything analogous to the *Aio te Æacida, Romanos vincere posse* of the historic oracle."

The opinion of a well-known American scientist respecting the advantage to be derived from a scientific study of astrology should not be without weight with those who are able to concede to others a degree of discrimination and discernment equal to that which they claim for themselves. The sober verdict of a trained scientific mind must surely carry more weight than the argument from "common sense," which is the chief weapon in the armoury of uninformed prejudice.

The late Professor Joseph Rodes Buchanan, scientist, physician, and author, who ended his life's labours in San Jose, California, at the age of eighty-five years, says in his book, "Periodicity," p. 31: "If I were now to give my best advice to a friend in his outset in life, I would advise him to get the advice of a scientific and honest master of astrology, who would show him the path of destiny which he has already trodden and must follow through life, either blindly stumbling or with his eyes open to all dangers.... I regret that I did not learn the value of the science in time. It would have saved me from serious errors."

Chaucer is full of astrological references, and the poet well knew the influence of the planets in the different signs of the zodiac—*i.e.*, as significators. In lines 10, 655-664 the effect of Mars rising in the sign Taurus (ruled by Venus) are well described:

> "For certes I am al Venerien
> In feeling, and my heart is Marcien;
> Venus me gaf my lust, my likerousnesse,
> And Mars gaf me my sturdy hardynesse.
> My ascendant was Taur, and Mars ther-inne.
> Allas! allas! that ever love was synne!
> I folwed ay myn inclinacioun,
> By vertu of my constellacioun.
> . . . . .
> Yet have I Marte's mark upon my face."
> . . . . .

The delineation is one that will commend itself to the student of astrology, particularly the *mark of Mars* referred to in the last line, it being a common observation that the presence of that planet in the ascendant of a nativity invariably produces a mark of some sort on the face, generally a mole or a scar.

Arthur Gilman, M.A., gives the following note on p. cxvi of the Introduction to his edition of Chaucer: "Mars being a wicked planet, it was inauspicious or which is the degree of the zodiac seen upon the Eastern horizon at the time of an observation." Any astrologer would confirm this statement, and, indeed, any student of astrology could not but remark the careful manner in which Mr. Gilman has represented the science.

This may, perhaps, be regarded as selected evidence in favour of a rational system of scientific foreknowledge, but that it is most distinctly favourable must, I think, be admitted; and having regard to the nature of the testimony as well as to the source of it, we cannot very well escape the conclusion that astrology, the science of futurity, is at least deserving of impartial examination.

Let us now turn to an argued survey of the foundations of this ancient science as presented by the late R. A. Proctor, the well-known astronomer and author.

R. A. PROCTOR ON ASTROLOGY

"We are apt to speak of astrology as though it were an altogether contemptible superstition, and to contemplate with pity those who believed in it in old times. And yet, if we consider the matter aright, we must concede, I think, that, of all the errors into which men have fallen in their desire to penetrate into futurity, astrology is the most respectable, one may even say the most reasonable. Indeed, all other methods of divination of which I ever heard are not worthy to be mentioned in company with astrology, which, delusion though it was, had yet a foundation in thoughts well worthy of consideration.

"The heavenly bodies *do* rule the fates of men and nations in the most unmistakable manner, seeing that, without the controlling and beneficent influences of the chief among those orbs—the Sun—every living creature on the Earth must perish. The ancients perceived that the Moon has so potent an influence on our world that the waters of the ocean rise and fall in unison with her apparent circling motion around the Earth. Seeing that two among the orbs which move upon the unchanging dome-sphere are thus potent in terrestrial influences, was it not natural that the other moving bodies known to the ancients should be thought to possess also their special powers?

"The Moon, seemingly less important than the Sun, not merely by reason of her less degree of splendour, but also because she performs her circuit of the star-sphere in a shorter interval of time, was seen to possess a powerful influence, but still far less important than that exerted by the Sun, or rather the many influences manifestly emanating from him. But other bodies travelled in yet wider circuits if their distances could be inferred from their periods of revolution. Was it not reasonable to suppose that the influences exerted by those slowly moving bodies might be even more potent than those of the Sun himself? Mars circling round the star-sphere in a period nearly twice as great as the Sun's, Jupiter in twelve years, and Saturn in twenty-nine, might well be thought to be rulers of superior dignity to the Sun, though less glorious in appearance; and since no obvious direct effects are produced by them as they change in position, it was natural to attribute to them influence more subtle but not the less potent.

"Thus was conceived the thought that the fortunes of every man born into the world depend on the position of the various planets at the moment of his birth. And if there was something artificial in the rules by which various influences were assigned to particular planets, or to particular aspects of the planets. it must be remembered that the system of astrology was formed gradually, and perhaps tentatively. Some influences may have been inferred from observed events, the fate of that king or chief guiding astrologers in assigning particular influences to such planetary aspects as were presented at the time of his nativity. Others may have been invented, and afterwards have found general acceptance because confirmed by some curious coincidences. In the long run, indeed, any series of experimental prediction must have led to some very surprising fulfilments—that is, to fulfilments which would have been exceedingly surprising if the corresponding predictions had been the only ones made by astrologers. Such instances, carefully collected, may at first have been used solely to improve the system of prediction.

"The astrologer may have been careful to separate the fulfilled from the unfulfilled predictions, and thus to establish a safe rule. For it must be remembered that, admitting the cardinal principle of astrology, the astrologer had every reason to believe that he could experimentally determine a true method of prediction. If the planets really rule the fate of each man, then we have only to calculate their position at the known time of any man's birth and to consider his fortunes to have facts whence to infer the manner in which their influence is excited. The study of one man's life would, of course, be altogether insufficient. But when the fortunes of many men were studied in this way, the astrologer, always supposing his first supposition right, would have materials from which to form a system of prediction.

"Go a step further. Select a body of the ablest men in a country, and let them carry out continuous studies of the heavens, carefully calculate nativities of every person of note, and even for every soul born in their country, and compare the events of each person's life with the planetary relations presented at his birth, it is manifest that a trustworthy system of prediction would in the long run be deduced by them if astrology have a real basis in fact.

"I do not say that astrologers always proceeded in this experimental manner. Doubtless in those days, as now, men of science were variously constituted; some being disposed to trust chiefly to observation, while others were ready to generalize, and yet others evolved theories from the depths of their moral consciousness.

"But we must not forget that astrology was originally a science, though a false one.* Grant the truth of its cardinal idea, and it had every right to this position. No office could be more important than that of the astrologer, no services could be more useful than those he was capable of rendering according to

---

* Here Proctor abandons argument for unqualified and, I think, illogical assertion. Richard Proctor never proved astrology false, nor could it be a science if it were false. Science is what we know of *facts*.—S.

his own belief, as well as that of those who employed him. It is only necessary to mention the history of astrology to perceive the estimation in which it was held in ancient times.

"As to the extreme antiquity of astrology it is perhaps needless to speak; indeed, its origin is so remote that we have only imperfect traditions respecting its earliest developments. . . . Philo asserts that Terah, the father of Abraham, was skilled in all that relates to astrology; and, according to Josephus, the Chaldean Berosus attributed to Abraham a profound knowledge of arithmetic, astrology, and astronomy, in which sciences he instructed the Egyptians. Diodorus Siculus says that the Heliadæ, or children of the Sun (that is, men from the East), excelled all other men in knowledge, particularly in the knowledge of the stars. One of this race, Actis (a ray), built Heliopolis, and named it after his father, the Sun. Thenceforward the Egyptians cultivated astrology with so much assiduity as to be considered its inventors. On the other hand, Tatius says that the Egyptians taught the Chaldeans astrology. The people of Thebais, according to Diodorus Siculus, claimed the power of predicting every future event with the utmost certainty; they also asserted that they were of all races the most ancient.

"However, we have both in Egypt and Assyria records far more satisfactory than these conflicting statements to prove the great antiquity of astrology, and the importance attached to it when it was regarded as a science. The Great Pyramid in Egypt was unquestionably an astronomical—that is (for in the science of the ancients the two terms were convertible), an astrological—building. The Birs Nimroud, supposed to be built on the ruins of the Tower of Babel, was also built for astrologers. The forms of these buildings testify to the astronomical purpose for which they were erected. The Great Pyramid, like the inferior buildings copied from it, was most carefully oriented—that is, the four sides were built facing exactly north, south, east, and west. The astronomical use of this arrangement is manifest. . . .

"If we consider the manner in which the study of science, for its own sake, has always been viewed by Oriental nations, we must admit that these great buildings and these elaborate and costly arrangements for continual observation were not intended to advance the science of astronomy. Only the hope that results of extreme value would be obtained by observing the heavenly bodies could have led the monarchs of Assyria and of older Egypt to make such lavish provision of money and labour for the erection and maintenance of astronomical observatories. So that, apart from the evidence we have of the astrological object of celestial observations in ancient times, we find, in the very nature of the buildings erected for observing the stars, the clearest proof that men in those times hoped to gain results of great value from such work.

"Now we know that neither the improvement of navigation nor increased exactness in the surveying of the Earth was aimed at by those who built those ancient observatories; the only conceivable object they can have had was the discovery of a perfectly trustworthy system of prediction from the study of the motions of the heavenly bodies. That such was their object is shown with equal clearness by the fact that such a system, according to their belief, was deduced from these observations, and was for ages accepted without question. . . . The tenacity, indeed, with which astrological ceremonies and superstitions have maintained their position, even among nations utterly rejecting star worship, and even in times when astronomy has altogether dispossessed astrology, indicates how wide and deep must have been the influence of those superstitions in remoter ages. Even now the hope on which astrological superstitions were based, the hope that we may one day learn to lift the veil concealing the future from our view, has not been altogether abandoned. The wiser (?) reject it as a superstition, but even the wisest have at one time or other felt its delusive influence."

This testimony by R. A. Proctor is all that is needed to establish the claim of astrology to be regarded as a science. I am personally wholly in accord with the author in the view that the wiser (in their own conceit) reject it as a superstition without so much as a cursory knowledge of its principles; but the *wisest* cannot be said to "have fallen under its delusive influence," since they are beyond delusions. I would not like to say that Claudius Ptolemy, Tycho, Kepler, and Newton, all confessed astrologers, were of a class liable to be swayed by delusions so much as some of their successors are swayed by prejudice. One cannot fail to recall in this connection the incisive reply of Sir Isaac Newton to Mr. Halley, of comet fame, when the latter presumed to reprove the great master for his belief in astrology. Newton turned his limpid blue eyes upon his censor and calmly said: "I have studied the subject, Mr. Halley. You have not." Nor must we forget that it was Kepler, who formulated the mathematical principles of the constitution of the solar system which were afterwards proved by Newton, who said: "A *most unfailing experience* of the course of mundane events in harmony with the changes occurring in the heavens *has instructed and compelled my unwilling belief*." These words of Kepler are not such as would be used by one who had fallen under an infatuation or delusion. They embody a sober conviction from experience altogether in keeping with the scientific reputation of this great genius, and it is arrant presumption on the part of uninformed critics of astrology to repudiate this dictum by ascribing the belief to delusion and superstition, or the remarkable predictions of astrologers to "coincidence." A little thought would convince the average mind that many coincidences make a law. The ignorant speak of laws as if they were compelling forces in the universe. They are, in fact, nothing but our mental perception of the correlated successiveness of events. Law is a mental concept, not a cosmic energy. It would also be seen that a single accredited prediction which was true as to time and nature of event would establish an *a priori* argument for the scientific value of astrology if it could be shown—as it certainly can—that the prediction was made from mathematical calculation of planetary configurations, and that the event predicted could not otherwise have been foretold. The position of the average intellect towards astrology was well defined by the late Professor Max Müller, editor of the "Sacred Books of the East," from the Clarendon Press, Oxford, when he affirmed that some of our greatest intellects of the present day are capable astrologers (he was probably thinking of Lord Chief Justice Young, Dr. Richard Garnett, LL.D., Curator of the British Museum, and author of "The Soul and the Stars," and others), but "few care to let their studies be known, *so great is the ignorance* which confounds a science requiring the highest education with that of the itinerant gipsy fortune-teller." Let us leave it at that, and pass on to other evidence. I would, however, add in passing that Dr. Garnett for some years contributed to *Coming Events*, then under my editorial, a series of very learned and wholly scientific observations altogether confirmatory of the general experience of professed astrologers. His book, "The Soul and the Stars," is a fine piece of analytical work based on Ptolemy's rules regarding mental development and character, abnormalities, insanity, etc.

ASTROLOGY IN SHAKESPEARE

Readers of "Shakespeare" seem to be unaware that the author was a Rosicrucian and, of course, a Mystic, who necessarily had a profound knowledge of astrologic lore. Now and again he mentions Pythagoras, and more than once refers to the harmony of the spheres, either directly or under a veil. Readers of "Sepharial's Manual of Astrology" will be reminded, on coming to the "Planetary Notes" (p. 69), of the poet's reference to the gamut, in giving an example of the ill-understood and defective music characteristic of the scene, as falling far short of the ideal "music of the spheres." The play is "The Taming of the Shrew," which is a mystery play. The only correct text is the folio of 1623, from which I quote, for "able editors" have done much to strip the text of mystic symbols. In Act III., Scene i., we have Lucentio, Hortensio, and Bianca discoursing on "heavenly harmony," "music," and "philosophy." Lucentio is a personification of Light, from *Lux, lucis*, light. Bianca, which means white, to signify Purity, is called Minerva—*i.e.*, Wisdom—by Lucentio. These two, Light and White Wisdom, blend, or are united in marriage at the end. Hortensio is the Mercury-Venus or Hermes-Aphrodite, a compound of sensual Knowledge and Love; and so is an Hermaphrodite.

In Act I., Hortensio is described as a woman, as "Hortensio, *sister* to Bianca"; and when Petruchio and Grumio appear before Hortensio's door, Grumio cries: "Help! mistress; help!" Hortensio is a name derived from *hortensis*, a gardener, or cultivator, an apt description of Mercury-Venus. The fiddle or lute on which the Mercury-Venus, or a compound of sensuous Love and Knowledge, discourses, is the sensual soul, and this Hermaphrodite requests Wisdom, or Bianca, to read its " gamut," which the poet playfully writes " gamouth," to signify that it is only cognisant of sensual, not celestial or silent harmony. Thus Bianca (called Minerva in Act I.) reads as follows the Hermaphrodite gamut:

> "Gamouth I am, the ground of all accord.
> *A re*, to plead to *Hortensio's* passion.
> *Bee-me*, Bianca, take him for thy lord.
> *C fa ut*, that loves with all affection.
> *D sol re*, one cliffe, two notes have I.
> *E la mi*, show pitty, or I die.
> Call you this gamouth? Tut, I like it not.
> Old fashions please me best; I am not so nice
> To change true rules for odd inventions."

It will be seen that, on reducing this Hermaphroditic " gamouth " or gamut to astrologic symbols, it only extends to the same number of notes as the *five* senses, and falls short of the mystic *seven* by the omission of two notes, most essential to complete the harmony of perfect Love. The five are:

A ♀, B ♃, C ☉, D ♄, E ☿.

Venus takes the lead, and is to plead for the Hermaphrodites. Bianca, or Wisdom, is to *be* Hermaphroditic, too, in taking the Hermaphrodite for its Lord of Divinity. Then it puts two notes into its hot affection: C ☉ (*fa ut*), the latter being the old Latin form, now put "do"; two (*sol re*) into the Saturnian cleff D ♄; and, of course, two (*la mi*) to the credit of Mercury. There is no G and no ♂ in this "gamut," and Wisdom knows that Diana and Mars are essential to the harmony of the spheres if Love is to be joyous and fruitful. It foresees that it cannot be united or wedded or bedded with Light (Lucentio) if Diana and Mars are excluded from exerting their influences. Thus Wisdom, as Bianca, is dissatisfied with Hermaphroditic music, and says, "old fashions please me best." To understand Shakespeare it is necessary to know the celestial laws, not only as described by Ptolemy, but as discoursed upon by the Mystics.

This brief study of this fragment of the play reveals the fact that whoever wrote the "Taming of the Shrew" was a close student of astrological symbolism. I have very little doubt that Francis Bacon, Lord Verulam, was both astrologer and Rosicrucian, because in his argument for establishing astrology (*astrologia sana*) as a recognized part of physics he uses the expressions and terminology peculiar to astrology, and concludes that "we must give up this method of censuring by the lump and bring things to the test of true or false." There can be little doubt that "the test" was beyond the patience of his times, as it is beyond that of the average mind to-day; but as we are in the habit of entrusting these researches to accredited men of intellect in other departments of knowledge, it is difficult to see what should prevent the public from accepting the conclusions from an exhaustive examination of this subject by those whose qualifications in other directions are beyond doubt.

Why should we accept the astronomy of Tycho, and Kepler and Newton, and not the astrology which they derive from it? Astronomy, to be of use to mankind, must finally be interpreted in terms of our daily life and thought, and astrology is the means whereby such interpretation is effected. You may cover your walls with facts concerning the distances, densities, masses, volumes, and motions of the planetary bodies, but unless you can determine the relations of these bodies to the race generally, and to yourself in particular, the facts are of no more use to you than the back page of last year's almanac.

Yet you are content to pay thousands of pounds sterling every year to have these facts repeated and added to by observers, recorders, calculators, and publishers. Solar physics have no meaning for the ordinary wayfarer. The appearance of a remarkable sporad of sunspots has an astronomical interest, but it only attains a human interest when we come to know what effect sunspots have upon the Earth itself, and thus upon ourselves as denizens of the planet. As a people we are too fond of and too reliant upon subsidized knowledge. We pay too much to have our thinking done for us. We prate a great deal about racial freedom and the liberty of the subject, but we remain by choice the slaves of the intellectually industrious. Consider for a moment what we take over on trust as "fact" in the upbuilding of our mental equipment. How many facts have we tested for ourselves? How much of our so-called knowledge is "home grown"? If we want to know the truth about astrology we must study it. Fortunately, the labours of many centuries are concreted in modern textbooks on the subject, so that the material for an impartial study of the subject is well in hand and accessible to the public at trivial cost. In an age of practical Democracy it behoves us to humanize our thought, and to interpret the facts of astronomy in terms of our daily life and common need. Failure to do this on the part of astronomers is the reason there are more astrological almanacs and ephemerides sold to the public than copies of the *Nautical Almanac*, from which they are constructed. The public are humanistic!

There is a touch of pure humanism, for instance, in the following note, which appeared in the *Illustrated London News* under the title of a "Scientific Superstition":

"It was a saying of some eminent person that there is no individual, however dull, from whom some information of a useful and interesting kind cannot be extracted. This strikes me as rather an optimistic view. However, I found it the other day corroborated.

I was talking to a casual acquaintance not much interested 'in music, poetry, and the fine arts,' and hazarded the remark that there had been a good deal of wind and rain in August. He looked at me with something very like contempt in his eye—and, indeed well he might. 'Well, of course,' he replied, 'there was a new Moon on Saturday, the 8th of August.' I said nothing, but thought to myself this is an even more foolish person than I imagined him to be. Now, dipping to-day into that interesting book, De Morgan's 'Budget of Paradoxes,' I came upon this very theory, not stated only to be ridiculed, but introduced for once as worthy of attention. Dr. Forster, the well-known meteorologist of Bruges, declares in the *Athenæum* of February 17, 1849, that by journals of the weather kept by his grandfather, father, and himself, ever since 1767, it is shown that, 'whenever the new Moon has fallen upon a Saturday, nineteen out of twenty of the following days are wet and windy.' This was corroborated by a number of correspondents to the same effect. One of them, who gives his name, writes that he has constantly heard this statement among the farmers and peasantry in Scotland, Ireland, and the North of England; that he has heard it remarked upon in the course of a seafaring life by American, French, and Spanish seamen, and even by a Chinese pilot who was once doing duty on board his vessel. De Morgan, of course, looked out for the next time the new Moon fell upon a Saturday, and found the fact to be to a great extent corroborated. There is no scientific reason to account for it; but at all events my friend was wiser than he looked, and much better informed than I was."

While not pinning my faith to the " casual acquaintance " whose observation elicited a reference to De Morgan's " Paradoxes," I can thoroughly appreciate the obvious humanism displayed by the journal which finds this sort of observation of interest to its readers. It is a tacit confession of the fact that popular interest is directly related to popular, and therefore unscientific, experience. The average man has more attention to bestow upon a statement of possible utility than upon the most recondite of scientific propositions remote from his daily life. Astrology in relation to the bread-and-butter question has its advocates.

Enough has probably been said to indicate my personal views in regard to the subject in discussion. A popular verdict would probably sustain my position, but that is not what I am now arguing for. I am asking for this ancient science the same impartial study and test as has hitherto been accorded by men of science to other important subjects. If there be any fundamental truth in the concept of planetary influence in human life, it is for men of science to extricate this from the overgrowth of superstition by which it may be said to be encumbered, to develop its possible uses and application along purely scientific lines, and thus to confer a double service on mankind. Left to itself, astrology will continue to grow upon the popular imagination, to make a stronger appeal to the credulous, and to become itself a menace to the world at large.

The civilization of popular knowledge is of paramount importance, and by this I mean its scientific, philosophical, and ethical rendering. And since neither persecution, nor legislation, nor ridicule has been effectual in suppressing the study of this ancient science, it remains only for science to take it in hand, and so deal with it as to render it capable of an intelligible and utilitarian expression. It has already been sufficiently shown that if there be logical or scientific grounds for repudiating the doctrines of astrology, those who follow it are erring in good company; but if neither logic nor science can accommodate the fact of scientific prediction, then so much the worse for those who condemn it without a trial. To the extent that intellectual vanity finds it convenient to contemn the truth, by so much is the truth held back against the day when its incontestible force will assert itself, to the dismay of the egotist and the wilfully blind.

There are some who think themselves to know better than their Master. He who said, "There shall be signs in the sun and moon and stars" of great international warfare, was not speaking at random, but in strict conformity with the covert agreement wherein the celestial bodies were appointed "for signs (signals) as well as for seasons and days and years, with the stars." To some of my readers it may appear a puerile thing to cite a popular notion of wet weather being connected with lunations falling on a Saturday. It is not, however, so inconsequent as might at first be supposed. It would puzzle some people to determine how often this coincidence occurs. The lunations fall on the same days of the month every nineteen years, roughly speaking, and the days of the week coincide with the same days of the month at irregular intervals affected by the interpolation of leap-year day, the series having been permanently fractured by the introduction of the Gregorian Calendar in 1582. It is clearly seen, however, that there is a definite periodicity arising from the employment of two periods of nineteen years and seven days respectively, and although it may become a local question as to where Saturday begins and ends, yet the popular observation in itself constitutes one of those "coincidences" which, when found to be continuously repeated, lead to the formulation of a law. The underlying causes are the legitimate inquiry of science, and for aught we know science may yet subscribe to a law of sequential electro-magnetic variation coincident with the days of the week. At present we can only advance astrological reasons why the days of the week are universally ordered as they are, and even these do not more than suggest why the first day was allotted to the Sun.

THE GREAT YEAR

THE ancients have frequently mentioned a period of time in which, according to their views of celestial motions, all planetary bodies return to a conjunction in the same portion of the ecliptic. This they called the *Annus Magnus*, or Great Year. Manilius, who was a skilful astrologer, and whose work on the influence of the signs of the zodiac has been translated into English, is said by Pliny to have maintained that this epoch (the commencement of the Great Year) " was reached at noon on the day when the vernal equinox occurred among the stars of Aries." Cicero writes to the same effect, and Plutarch also, that the Great Year would terminate when the ☉, ☽, and planets should return to the same sign whence they set out.

Commenting on this generally received idea of the *Annus Magnus*, Mr. Samuel Stuart, of Auckland, N.Z., has addressed a most interesting letter to the journal of the British Astronomical Association, in which he shows that the tables of Ptolemy were quite inadequate for any such retrospective calculation as that which seems to have been made by Manilius. It is true that the *Almagest* of Ptolemy, although the best work to which the second and third century writers had access, is faulty. But Plutarch, who wrote in the first century, could not have made his statement from knowledge of those tables.

Manilius, who wrote in the year 45 B.C., must have had a more profound knowledge of celestial motions than astronomers at that period are credited with. This fact is fully borne out by the following statement by Mr. Stuart:

THE GREAT YEAR

"By the aid of planetary cycles deduced from modern *data* we discover that the date wanted is 39,734 years prior to 1801 A.J.C. Then, if we set back the Julian date of 1801 by 100,000 years, it becomes 106,514, from which, taking 39,734, we have 66,780 as the year required. And on the day preceding the mean equinox, which was Friday, January 14, old style, or Friday, March 23, new style, in that year, according to the astronomical elements of Leverrier, a calculation of the mean geocentric places of the Sun and planets yields the following very curious results:

	Geoc. Long.		Geoc. Long.
Neptune	11° 9°	Mars	0° 2°
Uranus	0° 15°	Sun	11° 29°
Saturn	11° 19°	Venus	0° 27°
Jupiter	0° 25°	Mercury	11° 19°

♓ ——— ♈ ——— ♉

♆ ♀ ♄ ☉ ♂ ♅ ♃ ♀
9 15 19 29 2 15 25 27

And in reference to this singular position of the planets Mr. Stuart remarks:

"So far as the Sun and the five planets known to the ancients are concerned, the result looks strange enough; but the inclusion of Neptune and Uranus seems extraordinary. In any case, the calculations appear to show that the celestial positions which Plutarch seems to describe actually took place, and within a reasonable period of the date to which, in round numbers, he approximates. But if so much be granted, it would militate strongly against all that we know as to the astronomy of the ancients, and how they came by the knowledge of such a position might be a very interesting question."

The Hindus have a period of 4,320,000 years, which is the sum of the four *Yugas* or ages, and this number is said to be the least common multiple of the number of *days* required by the planetary motions to effect a return of all of them to the same sign of the zodiac.

The famous Naronic cycle of 600 years, multiplied by 12, the number of the signs of the zodiac, gives 7,200 years, and this period multiplied by 360, the number of degrees in the circle, yields 2,592,000 years, or 100 times the period anciently believed to be required for an entire precession of the equinoxes.

This period of 25,920 years is held to be the period in which the Sun performs one revolution in its orbit, and if the centre around which it is moving is, as some astronomers believe, the star Alcyone, or one in the same direction, then the Sun's mean radius vector is capable of being determined within certain limits. Thus, $R \oplus = 95,000,000$ miles, then $\frac{R \oplus \times 360°}{50''} = R \odot$, and this gives $2,462,420,000,000$ miles as the $\odot$'s radius vector.

But so far as the Great Year is concerned it is of importance to note that Manilius, the astrologer, the contemporary of Cicero, Cæsar, Virgil, Horace, and other great lights of the Roman Empire, was justified in his statement that the period was marked by the return of the planets with the Sun to the vernal equinox. Yet there are sober-minded people, who, while admiring the genius of such men as Manilius, Kepler, and others, cannot see in the astrological beliefs of these master-minds anything but error and superstition.

In connection with this period of 25,920 years it has to be observed that it is directly related to the mean precession of the equinoxes, which is $50''$ per year, and thus the circle is exactly 25,920 times this amount. This gives for each of the twelve signs a period of 2,130 years. Here we have a suggestion of the natural correspondence of a day, during which the heavens move through one degree, and the ancient year cycle of 360 days. Thus we get a direct interpretation of Daniel's " seventy weeks " or 490 days as 490 years; and we further see that the desolation of a " time, times, and a half time " of the Hebrew prophet is identical with that of "forty and two months," or 42 times 30 days in the prophecy of John of Patmos in the Revelations.

The prophets employed a primary solar cycle of thirty-six years during which the symbolism of a sign of the zodiac was dominant. Twelve such periods extending through a complete circle yields a period of 432 years, and a cycle of sixty such periods brings us again to the Great Year.

It should not escape attention that the Sun has a proper motion through space, and in all probability is answering to the gravitational pull of another great ion in the confines of space. A determination of the path of the Sun among the stars has led to the belief that this centre of attraction is in the direction of the star Alcyone in the Pleiades. However that may be, we have every reason to presume that the relative motion of the Sun follows Kepler's law of elliptical orbits, and in such case the solar system has aphelion or perihelion, and consequent variable acceleration, its motion at perihelion being greater than the mean, and at the aphelion less than the mean. Then, as the Sun is now passing through an arc of more than 50" per year, it must be nearer to its perihelion than to its aphelion at present time, if we are to accept Plato's measure of the Great Year as correct. Estimates of the cycle based on the present precession of the equinoxes necessarily give a period less than that of Plato.

To this observation we may add the following original note, which goes to show that Plato's expression, "God geometrizes," is not an empty phrase, but a profound philosophical and scientific statement.

If we take the two greatest bodies of the solar system, Jupiter and Saturn, whose combined masses are greater than those of all the other bodies of the system put together—excluding the Sun, of course—we find it not surprising that the ancients on this account regarded them as the chief chronocrators, and paid great attention to their conjunctions. Two periods of Saturn are found to be nearly equal to five of Jupiter —namely, sixty years. In 960 years the two bodies come into conjunction again in the same part of the heavens. If we divide the Great Year of 25,920 years by 960 we get exactly 27. This is the number of the asterisms or lunar "mansions" in use among the Chaldeans, Arabs, and Hindus. Each of these mansions are 13° 20' in extent, which is equal to 48,000", and this being divided by 960 gives 50" the value of the mean annual precession of the equinoxes. Thus—

$$As\ 25,920 : 360° :: 960 : 13°\ 20';$$
$$and\ as\ 960 : 13°\ 20' :: 1 : 50''.$$

If we apply this period of 960 to historical events we shall find that it appears to afford a striking analogy in the foundations of the old and new Germanic Empires. Thus the old Empire was founded by Conrad I. in A.D. 911, and exactly 960 later, in 1871, the new German Empire was founded. The Roman alliance was founded in A.D. 962, and it is therefore to the year 1922 that students of prophecy are looking for the alliance under the "second beast" prior to the great devastation.

The period of 432 years already mentioned in connection with the Great Year and the phenomenon of precession is at the root of the ancient Hindu Yugas, or ages, indicated in the *Vishnu Purana*, and called the *Satya*, *Treta*, *Dvapara*, and *Kali Yugas*, or, as we call them, the Gold, Silver, Copper, and Iron Ages. Their relative lengths follow a numerical series of $1, 2, 3, 4 = 10$, so that the entire *Kalpa* or cycle is 4,320. Thus—

1.	432 years	× 100 =	432,000	Kali.
2.	864	,, ,, =	864,000	Dvapara.
3.	1,296	,, ,, =	1,296,000	Treta.
4.	1,728	,, ,, =	1,728,000	Satya.
	4,320		4,320,000	Kalpa.

In close association with the precession of the equinoxes we have the phenomenon of the variation

THE GREAT YEAR

in the inclination of the Earth's axis or obliquity of the ecliptic, and from a variety of observations of the meridian altitude of stars made at different periods in the same locality it has been found that the mean diminution of the inclination is 50" per century, or exactly one-hundredth part of the precession, so that the entire revolution, if such may be presumed, would occupy a period of 2,592,000 years.

A *Manvantara* consists of four ages, divided into two periods each, one of which is on the downward, involutionary arc, and one on the upward evolutionary arc. A Manvantara is 4,320,000 years, thus divided:

864,000		Satya	▲	864,000
648,000		Treta	│	648,000
432,000		Dvapara	│	432,000
216,000	▼	Kali	│	216,000
2,160,000				2,160,000
Involution		4,320,000		Evolution
		Manvantara		

These are all astro-geological periods. Each age (*Yuga*) is again subdivided into four periods. We are now presumed to be in the 5,003rd year of the fifth Kali Yuga of this Manvantara, which, if I remember rightly, is the fifth Manvantara of the world, which totals 19,639,402 years up to A.D. 1900. But I may be in error as to this Manvantara being the fifth of the series, and it should therefore be received with caution.

From this apparently empirical order of the ages of the world we are able to deduce a sound astrological basis. The ancient belief that the universe was formed upon the hexad is part of the general concept of the geometry of things as revealed in the laws of crystallography and formularies of chemistry. Water always crystallizes at an angle of 60°, and this may have given rise to Thales' idea of the world having been produced from water, though it could not have informed him that water was a body capable of more chemical combinations than any other known to us. In effect, we have here the ancient symbol of the interlaced triangles, or "seal of Solomon," defining the sextile, trine, and opposition aspects of the celestial bodies when 60°, 120°, and 180° apart. If we multiply the years of the Iron Age, or Kali Yuga, by the centennial variation of obliquity ($4,320 \times 50''$) we get 60°, for the Dvapara Yuga, or Copper Age, 120°, and for the Treta, or Silver, 180°. This observation leads to many conclusions which may be developed in another place to greater advantage. The reader will hardly escape the obvious association of the sixty-year cycle in use among the Chinese and Aryans.

CELESTIAL DYNAMICS

The influence of the stars, as of the planets, has its basis in the electro-motorical effects exerted on the magnetism of the Earth, which in its turn influences the human organism, affecting its psycho-physiological functions according to the changes thereby effected in its radical or normal condition.

The electro-motorical effect of the Sun upon the Earth is responsible for the magnetic changes taking place in our globe. Recent experiments by Mitchin, Wilson, and Fitzgerald, have shown that Jupiter and some of the fixed stars also exert a perceptible influence, and this probably applies to all other celestial bodies whose influence has not yet been registered. By directing the rays of these bodies through a telescope on to a selenium plate, a comparison was made between their effects and that of a candle-light at a distance of 10 feet. Taking the candle-light as $=1$, Jupiter registered 3,272; the star Orionis, 0,685; Aldebaran, 0,279; Procyon, 0,261; and Cygni, 0,262. The influence of the planets and stars upon the Earth's electro-magnetic status is, therefore, a scientific fact.

That the local magnetic condition of the Earth has a direct effect upon the nervous system of man is apparently borne out by the clairvoyant faculty of the inhabitants of Skye, the Mull, Antrim, and the adjoining basalt territory, which is a centre of great magnetic intensity, as shown by the reports of the Royal Commission. I maintain a dependency of the two facts. In astrology we find the same truth illustrated, for it is commonly received that those who are born at midnight, or within two hours before or after it, are gifted with an extraordinary development of the psychic faculties, especially when the ☉ and ☿, but sometimes also the ☽ and ♄, are in conjunction in the nadir. Now modern science has shown that the maximum of magnetic intensity is registered at midnight. The accord of the two physical facts, that of magnetic intensity in reference to the sensitivity of the physical system of man, is thereby established. The Yakutes and Tschukutes also of Northern Siberia are known to fall into nightly somnambulism during about three months of the year, and by this circumstance they suffer extremely.

There can be little doubt that the variations of magnetic intensity are the cause of planetary influence, not the direct rays of the bodies concerned, since they are found to act when under the horizon. The planets act upon us in an indirect way by their modifying influence on the magneto-dynamical effect of the Sun upon the Earth's aura. We have an instrument which registers the effects of the Sun in the several houses of a horoscope—the compass needle. Its variations during the day and throughout the course of the year show the amount of its variation from the *mean magnetical meridian* of any country, and this variation is a proof of the Sun's influence in the celestial circle. The planets also exert an influence upon the magnetic needle, as is shown in the case of Venus; and so every particle of matter must be influenced by it, though not free, like a needle, to register the effect. The medium of this force is undoubtedly the magnetic aura of the Earth.

This aura was demonstrated to exist by Carl von Reichenbach, the discoverer of od and od-light—a form of electricity visible only to persons of high magnetic sensibility, and then only in the dark. The Rontgen rays, uran rays, etc., are only several forms of activity in this odylic substance, and those who have read " The Sensitive Man " will find nothing new in the X ray of recent discovery by our learned professor. Reichenbach's book runs into 700 or 800 pages in two volumes, and contains a marvellous description of the instruments and machines used by him to register the effects produced.

The second volume of this work contains a description of the Earth aura. All bodies are shown to have a magnetic aura, which appears like the rays of the spectrum. The human aura is stated to be like that of the crystal, both longitudinally and laterally. The colour at the head is blue, and at the feet dark red; the right side is of a bluish tint, the left more ruddy and yellow. The body being laid horizontally upon the ground, the head to the north along the magnetic meridian, the colours are then seen in their greatest brilliancy and purity, beginning with blue at the head, and passing through blue-green, dark green, light green, yellow, golden yellow, orange, and ending at the feet with red.

When, however, the body is turned horizontally upon its axis, so as to perform a circle, the original colours are no longer seen; but the blue at the head undergoes successive changes, receiving an admixture of other colours according to the angle of deflection from the meridian. These new colours are those of the twelve houses of the heavens, and are arranged in the following order:

East.—Grey, colourless.
  2nd.—Dark grey or blue-grey
  3rd.—Blue, with red stripes, violet.
North.—Blue.
  5th.—Dark green.
  6th.—Light green.
West.—Yellow.
  8th.—Golden yellow.
  9th.—Orange.
South.—Red.
  11th.—Violet-red
  12th.—Grey-red

It will be observed that blue, the most magnetic colour, coincides with the north, and midnight; red, the most electric, with the south, and midday; the neutral or colourless to the east, and the dawn; yellow, the most luminiferous, to the west, and sunset.

A man is in the closest magnetic relations with the Earth when lying on his back with his head to the north, or standing or sitting with his face to the south. The body is then harmoniously disposed to the magnetic aura of the Earth, and gains rest and strength.

It would be possible to carry out this research into the domain of music, showing by what means certain strains excite to action, certain others to repose, some to exaltation of the faculties, and others to passional effects, for there is a known relationship existing between colour and sound, and hence between sound and magnetic condition. But I have contented myself in the present monograph with a consideration of the scientific basis of primary astrologic concepts.

These notes by Mr. Albert Kniepf are of such remarkable interest that I have not hesitated to employ them fully in this general survey of the Science of Foreknowledge. It is only when we come to understand the relations of the individual to environment that we are capable of forming a just estimate of the complex of influences with which he has to contend in the effort at self-expression demanded of him by nature. Nor can it be said that the electro-magnetic condition of the Earth's atmosphere at any given time and place fulfils our idea of environment. Man is in relation with the whole amphisphere of worlds, and his greater environment cannot be said to be defined by the limits of the solar system, still less by the etherosphere of the planet Earth.

Assuming, however, that the scheme here unfolded correctly represents the electro-motorical effects of the Sun upon the Earth's etheric ambient, it is clear that the whole effect in any quarter of the heavens is due to the angle of incidence. For what we call east will at one and the same moment be south to a locality 90° east of us; so that in the suggested colour scheme the grey colourless Orient is changed to the red of the south. It is not, of course, suggested that the colour scheme is optical, but only that it represents the local variation of electro-magnetic conditions. It is not said whether these conditions are permanent in relation to any locality, or whether they assume activity only on the incidence of the solar rays. I should, however, be disposed to regard them as hypothetically fixed in relation to any place, and the impinging of the rays of successive planets in their ascensions, culminations, and settings would produce kaleidoscopic variations in the electrical field which might reasonably be held to have a direct influence in the production of the variations of individual temperament, physical development, etc., according to the conditions obtaining at the moment of birth. The theory affords a good working basis for a scientific apprehension of the *modus operandi* of planetary action, seeing that these alleged effects are not due to the action of the Sun alone, but of all the celestial bodies in the stellar ambient, and are not held to be the direct effects of such agents upon the individual, but the result of organic response to the conditions set up in the Earth's etheric photosphere by the action of these remote bodies of the same and allied systems.

The following astrological notes upon have known denizens of the solar system may prepare the way to a fuller consideration of some of the evidences for a science of foreknowledge.

NEPTUNE

From a perusal of the ephemeris of Neptune some general indication of the orbit of this body may be had.

1. The greatest south declination attained by the planet is 22° 24′, a position reached on September 27, 1823. From this we learn that the planet's orbit does not lie in the same plane as the ecliptic, but lies at a less obliquity within the tropics. When in declination 22° 24′ its longitude is the fifth degree of Capricorn.

2. It crosses the Equator when in the fourth degree of Aries, and the ecliptic in the twelfth degree of Aquarius, its greatest latitude being about the quadratures of Aquarius 12°.

Its least motion during a span of 100 years is 2° 6′ 49″, and its greatest about 2° 16′ per annum. Its mean annual geocentric motion taken for 100 years, from December 31, 1799, to December 31, 1899, works out at 2° 11′ 10·2″. But, taking the half of its period as 82 years 136 days, we obtain an annual motion of 2° 11′ 2·4″ per year, with a period of close upon $164\frac{3}{4}$ years.

The planet was discovered on September 18, 1846, by observation; but, theoretically, its position was approximately determined some months earlier.

The elements, as given by Leverrier, are as follows (January 1, 1850):

Long. in orbit	11ˢ 4° 33′ 7″
Long. of aphelion	7ˢ 15° 59′ 43″
Inclination of orbit	0ˢ 1° 47′ 2″
Eccentricity	0ˢ 0° 30′ 49″
Orbital revolution	164· years, 280·113 days.
Mean diurnal motion	0ˢ 0° 0′ 21·53″
Log. of half great axis	1·478696

NEPTUNE

From these elements its longitude and latitude at any date can be calculated. A satellite, for which the name of "Triton" was suggested by M. Camille Flammarion in 1879, is known to exist.

So much, then, for the astronomical relations of Neptune. We may now pass to a consideration of a mythology and astrology connected with this planet which, although physically unknown to the ancients, appears to have been in many respects remarkably anticipated by them.

In a note appearing in *Coming Events* incidental mention is made to the probable affinity of Neptune with the sign Capricornus. This statement I propose to support by reference to ancient mythology.

In the first place, it should be noted that Mr. H. S. Green, in his valuable contribution to the *Astrologer's Magazine* on the dignities of the planets, has formulated a scheme by which the planets have each two dignities, a "night" and a "day" house, the exaltations of the several planets being uniformly in the dexter sextile of their respective "night" signs. Thus it was suggested that ♃ had exaltation in ♑, and ♂ in ♍. Capricorn being dexter sextile to Pisces (the sign of Jupiter), and ♍ the dexter sextile of ♏ (the sign of Mars). Mr. Green found a singular harmony to pervade the system of planetary dignities when thus disposed, and my contention that ♃ was strong in ♑ and ♂ in ♍ was thus supported by the greatest test of truth—harmony.

In order to show that Neptune is related to the sign Capricornus, it will be necessary first to examine the nature of that sign, and next to demonstrate an affinity between the planet ♃ and Neptune.

1. The sign Capricornus is of a dual nature, and so represented in the planisphere of the Egyptians and the zodiacs of the Hindus. A goat with the tail of a fish is the figure which the ancients used to designate this half-terrene, half-aquatic character—a species of sea-horse or amphibian capable both on land and sea.

The Hindu name for Capricorn was Makara, from which, by transposition, the name Kumara, as applied to the sea-born gods, was derived. Now the sign Capricorn is ruled by Saturn, who was the father of both Jupiter and Neptune. Jupiter and Neptune were therefore brothers. Saturn (Chronos, Moloch, etc.) had the peculiar trick of devouring his young, and Time (Chronos) engulphs or devours all its products, at once the great producer and destroyer. When Ops gave birth to Neptune, Saturn devoured him. In other words, when the earthy trigon (♑, ♉, ♍) evolved a new magnetic potency, being thereby brought into cosmic relations with the newly created planet ♆, Saturn, the old-time ruler of the cardinal earthy sign Capricornus, absorbed the powers of that planet. But Metis, one of the Oceanides remarkable for her sagacity, gave Saturn a potion which caused him to disgorge his devoured offspring.

This Metis was the wife of Jupiter, and is astrologically synonymous with Mercury (in its female aspect). She was devoured by Jupiter, in fear lest she should produce a greater than he. Subsequently, Jupiter's head being split open, Metis emerged as Minerva, armed from head to foot. This Minerva is undoubtedly associated with Mercury (as the ruler of Virgo), for we find her disputing with Neptune (sign Pisces) concerning the naming of Athens. The gods decided that the one who should produce the best gift to mankind should have the prerogative. Neptune produced a horse (Sagittarius), while Minerva produced the olive.

It is a beautiful idea that the Goddess of War should produce the symbol of peace! But note, Minerva was the first who built a ship; she delighted in navigation, and was the patroness of the Argonauts. She placed the prophetic tree of Dodona behind the ship Argo (a constellation in the sign ♍), and was known as Argorea, because she presided over the markets. Indeed, a more versatile deity is not comprehended in the Greek pantheon than this prototype of the genius of Virgo. Mention of the name at once brings to mind the inviolability and absolute virginity of the goddess, a further evidence of her association with the sign Virgo and the planet Mercury.

When Neptune was born he was hidden away by his mother, who declared she had brought a colt into the world. So from the very outset Neptune is associated with the sign ♐, one of those attributed to Jupiter in practical astrology. Then, in the dispute cited above, he produced the horse as a gift to mankind. He was made ruler of the entire waters of the Earth, and his dominion was only equalled by that of Jove (Jupiter). He is represented as sitting in a chariot made of a sea-shell, drawn by sea-horses or dolphins, and because he obtained the love of Amphitrite by assuming the form of a dolphin he is said to have placed that constellation in the heavens.

It is here that we come upon the track of the sign Capricornus in association with Neptune. Amphitrite is the Moon in the astrological capacity of the "mistress of the sea," in connection with the sign Cancer. Daughter of Oceanus and Tethys, she became the wife of Neptune, who appeared as a Dolphin (Capricornus), and had a son called Triton, one of the sea-gods.*

2. If the student will refer to the celestial globe he will find as anti-scions of Capricornus, Indus (the Hindu) and Dolphinus. It is well known that the ruling sign of India is Capricornus, and that the sign is opposite to Cancer. Thus Neptune comes to be associated with horses, the ocean, the dolphin (seahorse), also all rivers, springs, fountains, and lakes, and thus with fishes. On the one hand we find a radical association with the signs ♐ and ♓, and on the other hand we have certain later developed affinities with the sign Capricornus ♑. Hence there are lines of connection with the planets ♃ and ♄,

* See note above on the satellite of Neptune.

instituted by means of their ruling signs, as we have already seen.

To Neptune the dominion of the sign ♓ has already been attributed by empirical art, and sympathetically the sign Sagittarius also becomes involved.

Among the Romans, the festival of Neptune was celebrated by a pageant of gaily caparisoned horses led through the streets. Then as to the connection with Capricorn, it should be noted that Ægæus was the surname given to Neptune, and that the *Ægæum mare* (now called the Archipelago) came so to be named by reason of ♑ Capricorn, the goat, or αιγες, being the ruling sign of Greece.

It will be remembered also that the Ægis, or goatskin shield adopted by Jupiter, is in agreement with the idea of ♑ being the exaltation sign of ♃.

When, therefore, we come to examine the evidence afforded by mythology, we are borne to the conclusion that between ♃ and ♆ there is a great sympathy, and that the signs ♓, ♐, and ♑ are those which properly may be regarded as the territory of these planets. Personally, I am disposed to give the dominion of ♐ to ♃, and that of ♓ to ♆, making the exaltation of ♃ to be ♑.

Later, it will be found that ♂ (Mars) will have to yield one of its signs to Pluto, as Saturn has already yielded one to Uranus (Ouranos), and Jupiter (♃) one to Neptune. But until Pluto is located beyond the orbit of Neptune we cannot do better than devote our closest attention to the nature and attributes of the ocean deity and his representative among the spheres.

Apart from the strong suggestion of deep occult knowledge by the ancients conveyed by these references to their mythology, it would appear that an empiricism to which they could not pretend in ignorance of the actual body of Neptune is altogether in support of their mysticism. Beyond this point we need not labour the question.

THE NEW SATELLITE—LILITH

The course of events in the lives of several hundreds of persons whose horoscopes have come under our notice has amply justified our diagnosis of the influence of Neptune in human life and thought. Its chaotic, nebulous, scheming, and seductive influence when afflicting the significators by conjunction or evil aspect; its neurotic and enthused character, bordering upon the insane; its inconstancy; its excitability; its love of watching and spying out secrets; its predisposition to homicidal mania and assassination, have found illustration in numerous and conspicuous instances, supplemented and confirmed by the experience of very many students.

On the other hand, the ethereal, intuitive, and inspirational nature of Neptune when in benefic aspect to the significators, or dominating the mind by its presence in the first, third, or ninth houses of the horoscope, has not escaped observation and comment.

That Neptune is a *malefic* planet is well shown by the effects of its conjunction and parallel with the significators at birth and by direction.

Its benefic aspects, like those of Saturn, Herschel, and Mars, are capable of conferring advantages and benefits in accord with the character of the planet and its radical import.

So far, then, experience has gone farther than mere surmise based upon the constitution of the higher gamut of the solar system, which supposes ♅ to have the same nature as ☿, and ♆ that of ♀.

This surmise is, in a measure, true, for no doubt ♅ and ♆ are the higher representatives of those minor planets; but the mere exaltation of faculty produced by Uranus and Neptune is sufficient to place their subjects outside the pale of convention, and so to set up a strain in the conditions of everyday life, all of which makes the natives of their influence to be like the planets themselves—*outrées*.

But whereas ♀ is a benefic in all worldly matters, Neptune, its prototype, is in all such matters a malefic, though in the higher regions of the mind its gifts are most manifest, and far more enduring than those of the fair goddess.

But now we come to a yet more novel ground of research. Dr. Waltemath, as everyone now knows, has definitely located the orbit of the second (? first) satellite of the Earth, whom we will here call, for convenience, *Lilith*. In his article to the *Globe*, February 7, 1898, he mentions various observations of this unrecognized member of the solar family, a number of which, taken for the dates of transit over the Sun's disc, enabled him to fix its synodical revolution at 177 days. We refer our readers to the *Globe* for further particulars concerning the satellite, and here reproduce the dates of observation referred to therein:

1. Lilith ☌ Sun   ..   .. June 6, 1761.
2.   ,,   ,, ... Nov. 19, 1762.
3.   ,,   ,, ... May 3, 1764.
4.   ,,   ,, ... June 11, 1855.
5.   ,, 148° elong. ..   .. Oct. 24, 1881.

Now, in order to establish the synodical revolution of Lilith it should be found that the number of days from one solar conjunction to another is a multiple of 177. This is actually so.

From June 6, 1761, to November 19, 1762, are 531 days = 177 × 3. From the latter date to May 3, 1764, are 531 days. From May 3, 1764, to June 11, 1855, are 33,276 days = 177 × 188, showing that after 188 complete revolutions its period is not affected by a single day. Now, as Waltemath points out,

177 days are six times the revolution of the Moon, or, as we may observe, one-half the lunar year of 354 days in use among the Hebrews.

From the synodical revolution of Lilith we are able to deduce its *mean diurnal motion* in the zodiac—viz., 3°—and as this motion coincides with its actual position after three revolutions, and after 188 revolutions, to within 30 minutes of longitude, it must be very exact.

We propose to use the symbol ☉ to indicate the orb we have, for astrological purposes, designated *Lilith*. It is now necessary to show how its longitude in any horoscope may be approximately determined.

1. Take any one of the dates when ☉ was ☌ ⊙, according to observation. These are:

   June 6, 1761
   Nov. 19, 1762
   May 3, 1764 } Epochs.
   June 11, 1855

2. Count the number of days from the epoch to the date of birth, allowing 365 days for common years and one day extra for each intervening leap year.

3. Divide the total number of days by 177, and the quotient will give the number of complete synodical revolutions, the remainder being the number of days expired since the last conjunction of Lilith and the Sun. If there be no remainder, the satellite is in conjunction with the Sun on the day of birth.

4. With the remainder, count that number of days from the date of epoch in the year of birth. This will bring you to the longitude of the ⊙ and ☉ at last conjunction.

5. Multiply the number of days from the day of last conjunction to the day of birth by three, and add that number of degrees to the longitude of the last conjunction. This will give the mean longitude of ☉ on the day of birth.

Thus, for May 8, 1864, we count from epoch May 8, 1764, to May 8, 1864; we obtain 36,525 days, which divided by 177, gives 206 revolutions and 63 days; and counting 63 days from May 3, 1864, backwards we find March 1, 1864, to be the date of the last conjunction, as may be seen in the Table of Conjunctions, which will greatly facilitate the calculations.

The ☉ is then in ♓ 11°, and 63×3=189° to be added to ♓ 11° for the longitude of Lilith on the given date, and ♓ 11°+189°=♍ 20°, longitude of Lilith, May 3, 1864.

Having obtained the approximate longitude of Lilith in a number of intimate horoscopes, the following observations should be made in order to obtain a knowledge of the normal characteristics and influence of the satellite.

1. In a horoscope of birth it should be found *void of aspects*.

2. Being thus uninfluenced, its normal effects on the affairs of the several houses may be known by its position alone.

3. To determine its influence on the mind, it should be found in conjunction with Mercury when ☿ has no other affections than those conferred by the *sign* it is in. Or ⊖ should be devoid of aspect, and in the third or ninth house of the horoscope.

4. Its effects on the body may be found by reference to the ascendant. The presence of ⊖ in the first house (and near the horizon), when void of aspect, would serve to show its physical peculiarities, if any.

N.B.—It is essential that ⊖ should be found *void of aspect*, or in ☌ with ☉, ☽, or ☿, when these latter significators are not otherwise affected. For obvious reasons, the □, ☍, ✶, and △ aspects are of no use towards determining the normal value of ⊖; since the □ and ☍ are always evil, the ✶ and △ good.

The next line of research in regard to Lilith is that afforded by directions and transits. Its approximate longitude can be brought to the mid-heaven, ascendant, or their aspects, by meridian distance and semi-arc measures in a rough manner, but before this can be done with any degree of accuracy a complete ephemeris of the satellite must be forthcoming. Meanwhile, I have every reason to think the Table of Conjunctions will enable students to proceed.

By secondary direction the satellite, as significator of ☾, can be directed at the rate of 3° for every year of life, and can also receive the ☌ and aspects of the planets in their secondary direction.

The transit of planets over the radical place of ⊖ should also afford some indication of its particular function in human affairs. New Moons falling on the degree held by Lilith at birth will afford yet further evidence in the required direction.

It may facilitate the calculation of Lilith's longitude to observe that in thirteen years it forms its conjunction with the Sun exactly thirty-one days later. The subjoined Table of Conjunctions, which I have calculated for a period of fifty-two years, will show the dates on which Lilith and the Sun are in the same geocentric longitude. It will be observed that a conjunction, as foretold by Dr. Waltemath, took place on February 2, 1898, and the next would take place at the end of July of that year.

So far as our experience extends—and at present it is necessarily inconsiderable—the effect of ⊖ is to produce rapid changes and upsets, and from a few instances under observation it would appear that Lilith's influence is somewhat like the Moon's, but not fortunate and more violent in its action.

In this connection it will be a matter of interest to know that an unrecognized scientist, Dr. Ziegler, an Alsatian, who was born in 1816, has noted the existence of an aeriform body in the orbit of the Earth whose period is taken as 121 days. This corresponds very closely to the satellite of Dr. Waltemath's discovery, the period of which is 119 days, its synodical period being 177 days.

The satellite Lilith returns to the same longitude on the same day in 126 years.

TABLE OF CONJUNCTIONS OF LILITH AND THE SUN.

Year	Date	Year	Date
1854	December 16.	1876	April 13.
1855	June 11.	,,	October 7.
,,	December 5.	1877	April 1.
1856	May 30.	,,	September 25.
,,	November 23.	1878	March 21.
1857	May 19.	,,	September 14.
,,	November 12.	1879	March 10.
1858	May 8.	,,	September 3.
,,	November 1.	1880	February 27.
1859	April 27.	,,	August 23.
,,	October 21.	1881	February 16.
1860	April 15.	,,	August 12.
,,	October 9.	1882	February 5.
1861	April 4.	,,	July 31.
,,	September 28.	1883	January 24.
1862	March 24.	,,	July 20.
,,	September 17.	1884	January 13.
1863	March 12.	,,	July 9.
,,	September 6.	1885	January 2.
1864	March 1.	,,	June 28.
,,	August 25.	,,	December 22.
1865	February 18.	1886	June 16.
,,	August 14.	,,	December 10.
1866	February 7.	1887	June 5.
,,	August 2.	,,	November 29.
1867	January 27.	1888	May 25.
,,	July 23.	,,	November 18.
1868	January 16.	1889	May 14.
,,	July 12.	,,	November 7.
1869	January 5.	1890	May 2.
,,	June 30.	,,	October 26.
,,	December 24.	1891	April 21.
1870	June 19.	,,	October 15.
,,	December 13.	1892	April 10.
1871	June 8.	,,	October 4.
,,	December 2.	1893	March 29.
1872	May 28.	,,	September 23.
,,	November 21.	1894	March 19.
1873	May 16.	,,	September 12.
,,	November 9.	1895	March 8.
1874	May 5.	,,	August 31.
,,	October 29.	1896	February 24.
1875	April 24.	,,	August 20.
,,	October 18.	1897	February 12.

TABLE OF CONJUNCTIONS OF LILITH AND THE SUN—continued.

1897	..	August 9.	1902	..	June 14.
1898	..	February 2.	,,	..	December 8.
,,	..	July 29.	1903	..	June 2.
1899	..	January 22.	,,	..	November 26.
,,	..	July 17.	1904	..	May 22.
1900	..	January 10.	,,	..	November 15.
,,	..	July 6.	1905	..	May 11.
,,	..	December 30.	,,	..	November 4.
1901	..	June 25.	1906	..	April 29.
,,	..	December 19.	,,	..	October 24.

The above Table of Conjunctions will facilitate the calculation of Lilith's longitude, inasmuch as the days elapsed since the last conjunction to the date of birth have only to be multiplied by three in order to obtain the number of degrees to be added to the longitude of conjunction to obtain the longitude at birth. The table can be extended right and left indefinitely by adding or subtracting (as required) 13 years and 81 days from the epochs in the first and last columns of the table. A conjunction of ☽ and ☉ does not infer a visible transit of the Sun's disc. It will depend upon the position of the satellite in its orbit at the time, and the inclination of the orbit to the plane of the ecliptic. All conjunctions of the Sun and Moon are not eclipses.

The unfolding of the higher gamut of planetary existence being so far satisfied by the discovery of ♅ the octave of ☿, ♆ the octave of ♀, and Lilith the second (? first) satellite of the ⊕, we may now look ahead in anticipation of the discovery of an octave of Mars. This, when discovered, will prove to be an extra-Neptunian planet of great dimensions but small density. It may be called Pluto, Lord of the Pit, Lord of Destruction, etc., according to the fancy of astrologers; but its functions will be those of Mars on the grand scale, and its place at the date 1914 will link it directly with the indications of the Great War.

A THIRD EARTH-MOON

THE following interesting facts have been communicated by Dr. Waltemath, the learned discoverer of the Earth's second satellite, which we have called Lilith. There is every reason to believe that a further and *third* Moon of the Earth exists—that is to say, besides the nocturnal luminary of which we are well assured, there are two others, one of which has already been accurately localized by Dr. Waltemath, and provisionally named by ourselves for astrological purposes; the other being under observation and probably identical with the body localized by Ziegler.

On February 16, 1897, at München, and also at Stuttgart, from 8.45 a.m. to 12.45 p.m. (a space of four hours), there was seen a dark body passing over the Sun's disc, its apparent diameter being one-tenth of the Sun's. Dr. Waltemath is of opinion that this body is identical with one seen at Berlin at about 5 a.m. on January 21, 1898. It will be observed that it coincides to within three days of our approximate ephemeris of the solar conjunction of Lilith, which gives February 13, 1897.

But the following singular event seems to invalidate the supposition of its identity with Lilith: On February 4, 1898, two Moons were seen, says Dr. Waltemath, one at Wiesbaden at 8.15 a.m., on the lower limb of the Sun—this was Lilith; the other at Greifswald at 1.30 p.m. This was observed by Poste-Director Ziegler and eleven other persons. This is the Third Moon.

Dr. Waltemath observed a body in October, 1897, and he thinks it was probably this Third Moon of the

Earth. It was rising when observed about 10 p.m. (at Hamburg) on October 6, 1897, and its zodiacal position was 77° long. 4° 9′ N. lat.

Richard Proctor was of opinion that there existed certain non-luminous bodies moving round the Earth in its orbit, and this idea seems to be borne out in fact, since such bodies have been repeatedly observed, and are even now under scrutiny. Esotericists seem to require the existence of such bodies in their concept of the Earth chain—bodies which may be regarded as the grandmothers and great-grandmothers of our globe, as the Moon is its mother, the former habitations of the Earth's humanity. The idea is not preposterous when taken with the concept of reincarnation, since such non-luminous bodies still persevere in their old paths, and even the Moon, although luminous, is little more in itself than an old and abandoned lime-kiln.

I am not yet in possession of sufficient facts regarding the Third Moon to give my readers any adequate notion of its movements in the zodiac, but if it be the body observed by Dr. Waltemath in 1897 it will have a synodical revolution of about 354 days, double that of Lilith, whose elements are already so well known that Dr. Waltemath was able to predict the date and position of its solar transit.

It is of consequence to observe that the conjunctions of Lilith and the Sun are given in our table on the supposition of a constant and uniform motion of 3° per day. From the recent observation of the body, however, as well as others previously recorded, it is evident that it's motion, like that of the Moon, is variable. Thus, on September 4, 1879, at North Lewisburg, Ohio, Gowey observed the body of Lilith in conjunction with the Sun. Our table gives the conjunction as on September 3, and Ohio being west of Greenwich, the table is one day out.

Again, the body of Lilith was in transit over the Sun's disc on February 4, 1898, and the table shows

February 2 as the date of conjunction, which is only correct within two days.

The following observations of the body seem to support the main arguments of Dr. Waltemath as to the period of Lilith, its appearance, etc.:

OBSERVATIONS OF EARTH SATELLITES.

1618.—September 2, by Riccioli, as a fiery red globe, eleven days before its opposition. Recorded in *Almagestum Novum*, vol. ii., p. 16.

1700.—November 7, by Cassini (the father) and Maraldi, at Montpellier. Recorded in *Memoires de l'Académie*, 1701.

1719.—December 23, in Hungary, five days before the opposition, a body was seen " like a red Sun with a white line across it."

1720.—March 27, by Dr. Alischer, at Fauer. ☊ ☌ ☉.

1721.—March 15, by Dr. Alischer, at Fauer. ☊ ☌ ☉.

1735.—June 29, by the Rev. Ziegler, at Gotha, three days before the opposition, as " an ample Sun of the night." Painted and published in pamphlet by Ziegler.

1761.—June 6, by anonymous writer to *London Chronicle*, at St. Neots, Huntingdonshire. ☊ ☌ ☉.

1762.—November 19, by Lichtenberg and Söllnitz, travelling to Erlangen. ☋ ☌ ☉.

1764.—May 3, by Hoffman, near Gotha. ☊ ☌ ☉.

1784.—March 25, by Superintendent Fritzsch, at Quedlinburg (*vide* " Bode's Astron. Alk.," 1805).

1855.—June 11, by Dr. Ritter, of Hanover, while travelling to Naples. A round black body was seen crossing the Sun's disc from west to east. ☊ ☌ ☉.

1879.—September 4, by Gowey, at North Lewisburg, Ohio. Recorded in *Monthly Weather Review* of the United States. ☊ ☌ ☉.

1897.—February 16, at München and Stuttgart, a dark body on the Sun's disc.

1898.—February 4, seen at Wiesbaden as a dark body transiting the Sun's south limb at 8.15 a.m. On same day, 1.30 p.m., at Greifswald, by Ziegler and

A THIRD EARTH-MOON

eleven other persons. A dark body on the Sun's disc.

A comparison of these dates and observations with the Table of Mean Conjunctions will, I think, convince any impartial person of the fact that a second satellite of the Earth certainly does exist, and that there is probably a third body in similar relations with the Earth as the Moon, which for ages has held undisputed sway as the Queen of Night.

The name Lilith suggested by me has been adopted for the Earth's second satellite. The following fact has some astrologic interest: The publication of the discovery of the satellite was made on January 22. 1898, the day of the ecliptic conjunction of the Sun and Moon in the sign ♒ (Aquarius), that ruling Hamburg, the town in which the publication was made by Dr. Waltemath. The eclipsed luminary was in close ✶ aspect to ♅, and △ to ♃, which greatly favours the reception of the discoverer's statement in scientific circles.

THE ASTROLOGY OF LILITH

In the foregoing pages, the substance of which appeared in 1898, I have cited a number of observations of Earth satellites supplied to me by Dr. Waltemath. It will be observed that many of the dates are those of the satellite Lilith's conjunction with the Sun. Its return to the *same* longitude on the *same* day, taking place every 126 years, makes the process of identification very simple. Thus we find an observation of Lilith ☌ ☉ on March 27, 1720, by Dr. Alischer, at Fauer. Now 1720+126=1846. This date does not enter into our Table of Conjunctions, but the table may be extended right and left by the addition or subtraction of 13 years and 31 days. So, if we add 13 years 31 days to March 27, 1846, we obtain April 27, 1859, which is the date of a conjunction of Lilith and the Sun as found in the table. Therefore, the observation by Dr. Alischer in 1720 was a transit of Lilith over the Sun's disc. Again, observation March 15, 1721, is identified in the Table of Conjunctions by the addition of 126 years and 13 years 31 days=139 years 31 days, which brings us to April 15, 1860, where we find ☾ ☉ ☌.

The observation of June 6, 1761, at St. Neots, by an anonymous writer to the *London Chronicle*, is at once identified by the addition of 126 years, which yields June 6, 1887, as found in the table under the previous day.

In 1762, on November 19, a transit of ☾ over the ☉'s disc was observed by Lichtenberg and Söllnitz travelling to Erlangen. This is found in the table as November 18, 1888. The observation of May 8,

1764, by Hoffman, near Gotha, is found in the table on May 2, 1890.

The conjunction given in the table on March 12, 1863, should be altered to March 13. The rest of the dates are taken out correctly for a mean synodical revolution of 177 days, which experiment has shown to be fairly exact. Having proved the existence of the satellite, we may presume an influence so long as it remains in relation with the Earth.

The influence of Lilith is undoubtedly obstructive and fatal, productive of various forms of catastrophes and accidents, sudden upsets, changes, and states of confusion. Falling in the fifth house of a horoscope, it has been found to indicate the insanity and death of a lover, loss of children, and death by childbirth. In the third house, it has signified accidents and death to brothers and sisters, and a series of troubles arising out of correspondence. In four cases under observation, the presence of Lilith in the sixth house has produced dangerous occupation ending in fatality.

The name Lilith comes from the Hebrew word *Lilah*, which means the Night. Dr. Wynn Westcott, the well-known author of several treatises upon Rabbinical literature, and especially reputable as the exponent of the Kabalistic notions of the Hebrews, has the following notes upon the Spirit *Lilith*, or *Lilis*, as derived through Semitic traditions: " Concerning Lilith, or Lilis, there is an immense collection of fables. In some she is a woman of pre-Adamic race, whom Adam found, and she was his first wife, and she begat demons. In others she is a Queen Demon, who seduces Adam and brings forth devils. Again, she is a general succubus at all times. Another idea is that she is constantly on the watch to do evil to the new-born babe who is not protected by Jewish theological rites. Again, that she is a vampire always seeking to kill infants; and again, that she seeks to kill men also, and that no man is safe who sleeps in a house alone, for he may thus be captured as Adam was.

She is also commonly called the wife of Samael and the mother of Shedim, and she ensnares. Lilith means a dust-cloud, but is also translated as Owl, and as a Screeching Bird of Night."

In the "Secret Doctrine" it is stated that "the third and fourth races became tall with pride: 'We are kings,' it was said, 'we are gods.' They took wives fair to look at, wives from the mindless, the narrow-headed. They bred monsters, wicked demons, male and female. Also *Liliths* with little minds." The Rabbinical stories about Lilith would appear to have come down from the Lemurian and Atlantean ages. These "giants of the Earth," who were primarily "sons of God," mind-born, took to themselves the "daughters of man," those who had come up along the line of physical evolution to the human-animal stage, but were without the spiritual inspiration which made of the Adamic race "living souls." Hence they were called the "mindless," though possessing natural intelligence derived from instinct, passion, and commerce with material things. They were of the pre-Adamic evolution, and their progeny from the sons of Mind was of the nature of Lilith, Rákshasas, Dákini, ghouls, demons, of the kind commonly known as incubi and succubi.

This note is of remarkable significance, inasmuch as it confirms the astrological character of Dr. Waltemath's second Earth satellite, which, for reasons I cannot here enter into, I at once christened Lilith. Suffice it to say that both in the East and West the dark, seldom visible, and mysterious "Eighth Sphere" is traditionally known. But more to our purpose is the fact that a considerable research already made has revealed the influence of Lilith (the satellite) to be just that which the Hebrews ascribed to Lilith (the mother of devils). The name is derived from Lilah (*Hebrew*, the night), and just as Adam was overcome by Lilith, so Samson was overcome by his Philistine wife, De-lilah.

Those who understand that a myth is a veil will not be content to scan the literal tradition, but will further seek to know and understand what truth lies behind the veil.

Let us now look at some of the astrological facts.

The following instances of young men who lost their lives while following their respective occupations have been sent to me from the Newcastle Colliery. The times of birth are all authentic, having been given to my correspondent by the parents themselves, and as they offer some interesting points for the student, I venture to bring them forward in detail.

No. 1.—Born August 5, 1863, at 4.55 p.m. Killed in the Seaham Colliery explosion by pit-fire September 8, 1880.

I find by calculation that the 29th degree of ♎ is on the meridian at birth, and the 23rd degree of ♐ rising. The following are the places of the planets at the time of birth:

☉ 12 ♌ 43	☽ 4 ♉ 10	♆ 5 ♈ 56	♅ 23 ♊ 49	♄ 2 ♎ 5
♃ 21 ♎ 11	♂ 1 ♍ 14	♀ 27 ♍ 14	☿ 15° ♌ 20′	☋ 7° ♊

The ☽ is found in the fourth house in the fixed and earthy sign ♉ in □ to ☉, and ♆ in ♌ in the eighth house, and the ascendant is opposed by the exact aspect of ♅. Lilith holds the cusp of the sixth house in the airy sign ♊. These are the immediate signs of danger in connection with the occupation of a collier.

Lilith causes rapid changes and upsets, its influence being unfortunate and violent, disruptive and fatal.

On September 8, 1880, the native was killed in the Seaham Colliery explosion, or rather by pit-fire following upon the explosion. His age was then 17 years 1 month. The ☽ had progressed to 5° ♐ 51′, and was therefore on the cusp of the twelfth house (the house of imprisonment and restraint) in close ☊ to ⊕ (Lilith).

The ☉ in the eighth house is posited in the fiery sign ♌, and 17 days after birth is found in declination 11° N. 53', which is that of ♂ at birth, another indication of "fire." The planet ♂ had progressed to 12° ♍ 37', and the new Moon of September 5, 1880, fell exactly on this progressive place of Mars! There was also an eclipse of the Sun on August 7, 1880, which fell within 2° of the place of the ☉ at birth. The ephemeris for September 8, 1880, shows ♄ in exact opposition to the meridian of the horoscope.

No. 2.—Born August 9, 1861, at 1 p.m., near Berwick. A stoker on a locomotive; he was killed by a truck falling upon him from a siding on December 30, 1887.

The 1st degree of ♍ was on the meridian at birth, and the 12th of ♏ was rising.

The planets were placed as follows:

☉ 16° ♌ 51'	☽ 26° ♍ 31'	♆ 1° ♈ 19'	♅ 15° ♊ 37'	♄ 9° ♍ 32
♃ 3° ♍ 0'	♂ 22° ♌ 39	♀ 11° ♍ 5'	☿ 28° ♋ 9'	⊕ ♉ 5°

It will be seen that the mid-heaven of the horoscope is occupied by ♃, ♀, ♄, and ☽, all in the sign ♍. The ☉ in the ninth house in the fiery sign ♌ is in conjunction (☌) with ♂ (Mars), a fiery planet, a very fitting indication of his occupation as stoker. The ☽ is approaching the ☍ of ♆. Here again we find Lilith in the sixth house, denoting dangerous occupation, a fatal service!

At the time of the fatal accident, the native was 26 years and nearly five months old. On the twenty-sixth day after birth we find the ☉ in ☌ with ♄ and ☿, and ♂ ☌ ♃, all in the sign ♍, the ☉ also applying to the square aspect of ♅ in ♊ in the eighth house.

THE ASTROLOGY OF LILITH

In December, 1887, the ☽ came by *direction* to a conjunction of the ☉ and ♄ in the mid-heaven of the horoscope, having lately passed the ☌ of ♂ and ♃. The direction is *exact*, and measures closely to the time of the accident. Yet there are really sober people who seriously deny the validity or the efficacy of "secondary" directions! To my mind, the obscuring of mental faculties which led to the accident are well accounted for by the ☌ of ♂ and ♃, and of ♀ with the planet ♄ by direction.

In 1887 there was an eclipse of the ☽ in the 19th degree of ♌ close to the ☉ at birth in ♌ 17°.

No. 3.—Born September 12, 1871, at 8 a.m.; was a seafaring engineer. Fell overboard a steamer on August 22, 1897, and was drowned.

My correspondent writes: "This case, so far as I can see, affords no indication of his untimely death. His father, who is well informed in astrology, showed the horoscope to me. We anticipated nothing but a successful future. His father declared that, had the horoscope shown any indications of death at twenty-six years of age, he would have kept him at home."

At birth, the 20th degree of ♋ (Cancer) culminates, and the 14th of ♎ (Libra) rises.

The planets are posited as follows:

☉ 19° ♍ 5'	☽ 19° ♌ 14'	♆ 23° ♈ 33'	♅ 29° ♋ 57'	♄ 3° ♑ 18'
♃ 23° ♋ 43'	♂ 19° ♏ 45'	♀ 9° ♎ 50'	☿ 29° ♍ 45'	☊ ♈ 6°

It will be at once noticed that, although ♃ holds the meridian of the horoscope and ♀ is not far from the eastern horizon, yet ♃ is afflicted by the near conjunction of ♅, ☋, and ♀ by □ ♄, and ☍ ☊. Here again we find Lilith in the sixth house, a most singular coincidence, surely! And here, too, it indicates danger in the occupation, and employment that is fatal. The Moon is hyleg in this horoscope, and is found in the sign ♌ in □ to ♂ in ♏, and in exact parallel with that planet.

These significators are in *fixed* signs, which predispose to drowning or suffocation.

Twenty-six days after birth, corresponding to twenty-six years of life, the ☉ has progressed to a ☌ with the ascendant at birth. The ☽ at 7.20 a.m. on the twenty-sixth day (corresponding to August 22, 1897) is on the place of ♅ P. in ♌ 0° 52'. The ascendant is directed to the □ aspect of ♅ in ♏ 0° 52'.

The indications herein are certainly somewhat inadequate, for although at birth the ☽ is □ ♂, it is elevated above ♂, and ♃ holds the mid-heaven in the ocean sign ♋ (Cancer), while ♀ safeguards the ascendant by its proximity to and rulership of that point. The ☉, it is true, has an approximate ∠ aspect of ♅, but it also has ⚹ of ♃, and this latter planet is essentially and accidentally dignified—*i.e.*, in regard to both its zodiacal and mundane positions.

It should not escape notice that the Moon is in the sign ♌ in a house, the eleventh, that corresponds to ♒ (Aquarius), and ♂ is in ♏ in the second house, normally that of ♉, so that the involved signs, being in opposition houses, and, indeed, *the whole horoscope being inverted* in respect to the natural zodiac, may in some sense have portended such a catastrophe as that by which the native lost his life.

Venus, the prime significator of the native, is badly afflicted by the ∠ ☽, □ ♄, and ☍ ⊖ (Lilith), this latter body being in the sixth house, as was hitherto remarked in the preceding cases, in each of which the occupation proved fatal. This circumstance should have record in the student's notebook, for we shall have to watch the newly discovered satellite very closely for some time to come.

Émile Zola had ⊖ in ♐ 8° at birth, and in 1898 the ☉ was directed *to the exact ☍ of that dark satellite*, and ♄ at the time of the Dreyfus *débâcle*, instituted by Zola in the winter of 1897, was in ☌ with the place of Lilith at birth.

In Queen Alexandra's horoscope Lilith is in the fifth house, in ♓ 19°, and the Duke of Clarence (her first-born) died at twenty-eight years of age, when ☉ was directed to ☍ M.C. in the Queen's horoscope.

It is an important factor, inasmuch as ♃ holds the fifth house in its own sign ♓, and hence would suggest long life and good fortune to the first-born. Lilith, however, negatives this influence by its *nearer position to the cusp* of the fifth. Comparing this with the horoscope of a lady born January 29, 1864, at 8.10 p.m., London, we find ♃ in ♏ in the fifth house, but ☉ in ♐ 5 also in the fifth. She had daughters born, but the first male child died.

The one time popular actor, Win Terris (Lewin), had ☉ in the tenth house in ♑ 16°, ∠ ☉ on the cusp of the twelfth. He led a roaming life, followed many pursuits, and died a violent death.

The Tsar of Russia, Nicholas II., has the satellite at birth in the fifth house, in ♒ 5°, and it will therefore be interesting to mark the destiny of his first-born son, in whose horoscope the Sun is opposed by Saturn.

The Kaiser Wilhelm II. has Lilith in ♋ 80° in the ascendant of his horoscope, a further indication of the evil destiny of this monarch.

The horoscope of King George V. shows ☉ in the 15th degree of Capricorn, and therefore in the tenth house, an indication of great political changes and revolutions in the course of his reign.

It would be possible to extend these observations indefinitely, but probably enough has been said to indicate that the nature of Lilith is violent and subversive, destructive and sinister. Its position at birth of an individual will show what dangers are signalled, according to the "house" or division of the heavens in which it is found. By means of the Table of Mean Conjunctions its position may be calculated in all known horoscopes, and a valuable series of observations may be thence made.

INDIAN ASTROLOGY

It has been asserted that "we can find a dozen writers who allege that the Hindus get their astrology from Chaldea and Egypt, but n t one authority can we find who controverts this." Frankly, I should like to examine the credentials of these twelve "authorities." I am prepared to find that not one of them has familiarity with the subject of astrology, either European or Hindu. My personal intercourse with the Jyotish' shástris (astrological experts) and pandits of India confirmed me in this belief, and what I have seen of the work of the Orientalists does not impress me to the contrary.

When the "Suryasiddhanta" has been closely studied from first to last, the Orientalist is as far from any conception of the basic principles of Jyotish vedanga (astrology) as a new-born babe. Bailly has given us a very good rendering of the astronomy of the Hindus in his "Astronomie Indienne," but he and all other Orientalists are silent on the subject of Hindu astrology. The fact is that, never having touched the subject in their own language, they wisely refrain from involving themselves in the more intricate system of the East as expounded in the Sanskrit Shástras.

Though no "authority" from a mere linguistic point of view, I venture to controvert the dictum of those twelve writers who allege (but do not prove) that the Hindus got their astrology from either Chaldea or Egypt. I will advance my arguments against this allegation.

1. No Orientalist has yet disposed of the fact that Sanskrit is the oldest Indo-European language, the

parent language of the Aryan race. None has shown, nor can show, that Accadian, the principal language of the ancient Babylonians, is of greater antiquity than the Sanskrit, or the Babylonians more ancient than the Aryans. The language of any people is the direct outcome of its thought, for it is embodied thought, and hence expresses all those particulars and peculiarities of environment which induced the thought of the people, their religious beliefs, their social polity, and all that goes to make up the round of their lives. Such is the Sanskrit in which the Vedas are written. And of Sanskrit it may be said without fear of contradiction that it is at once the most complex, complete, and highly inflected language within our knowledge. The Chaldean and Hebrew tongues are in comparison with it as the lisping prattle of a child is to the mature diction of a philosopher. The astrology of the Hindus is all written in Sanskrit. Translations have been made into the vernaculars, into Hindi, Telegu, Tamil, Mahratti, Kanarese, but all primarily are traceable to the teachings of the Hindu sages, Narada, Garga, Párashara, Vahara Mihira, and others.

2. It is true that India, under the Princes, enjoyed a free commerce with the surrounding nations, and that certain traditions may have passed current among men. But we have to remember that this commerce was restricted to one caste of the Hindus— viz., the Vaishya, or merchant men. The landlord was never allowed to travel out of his country. Yet it is these Brahmins who, as hereditary shástris, are responsible for the entire Jyotish' shástra. Even at this day it is only the Brahman who is permitted to expound the Vedas, and previous to the invasion of India by foreign nations the literature of the country was exclusively in the hands of the Brahmans.

3. If Claudius Ptolemy derived his astrology from the Chaldeans, or if the methods advocated as original with the Chaldeans had any tradition in Egypt, certain

it is that neither Chaldean nor Egyptian astrology had tradition in India, for the sole and sufficient reason that the astrological methods of the Hindus are essentially and fundamentally different to all that is reputed Chaldean and Egyptian.

In the first place, their zodiac is not related to the equinox, but counts from the fixed star Revati, which is now about 19° 35′ 17″ east of the vernal equinox.* The calculation of periods is based on the twenty-seven Nakshatras, or asterisms, and are reckoned from the place of the Moon at birth. What we called "Chaldean Directions," based on the diurnal aspects of the planets after birth, form no part of Hindu astrology. How, then, can it be said that the father has been taught by his children?

It must not be thought that because the Hindus do not relate their zodiac to the equinox they were ignorant of those considerations which determine our Western methods. They were, apparently, well informed concerning the procession of the equinoxes and solstices, and the proper motion of the stars. They knew how to make fairly accurate observations, and did not neglect the study of astronomy. The "Kalasankalita" tables show this to be the case.

In Varaha Mihira's work, entitled "Brihat Samhitá," there is a passage which not only determines the date of that writer, but also that of Paráshara, whom he quotes. Mihira says: "The summer solstice is now in the first point of Kátakam, and the winter solstice in Makaram, but the summer solstice was at one time in the middle of Aslesha according to former writers." Kátakam is the constellation of Cancer; Makaram is Capricornus; Aslesha is Leo. From this we learn that the *constellation* of Aries corresponded with the *sign* Aries when Mihira wrote his treatise on astrology—viz., in the year A.D. 498—and also that observations

* Mr. B. Suryanarain Row makes the Ayanamsha 21° 44′ 47″. I have used the epoch K.Y. 3,600 as given in the "Kalasankalita" tables. Procession = 50¼″ per annum.—S.

had been made over 2,000 years before that date, when Taurus was an equinoctial and Leo a solstitial constellation. The two zodiacs are distinguished by the Hindus by the names of *Sayana* and *Niryana*, that which has motion and that which has none. It is well known that at the beginning of the year the worship of Maya under the figure of the Bull (Apis) was performed by the Egyptians in the month of May, in honour of the Sun's entry into the constellation Taurus, the solar disc between the bull's horns being emblematic of the astronomical fact.

The Hebrews must have witnessed this ceremony during their captivity in Egypt, since they sought to perpetuate the custom in the worship of the golden calf after their exodus. The incident is in accord with the astronomical fact, for the Sun came to the equinoctial point in the constellation Taurus during the period of the captivity. It is evident, however, that the celebration continued with the Egyptians after the equinoctial point had left Taurus and had passed into Aries, for Moses, who was "learned in all the lore and language of the Egyptians," put the Hebrews straight in this matter by instituting the Pasach (transit), or Passover, to coincide with the true equinox. He prohibited the worship of the Bull, and instituted the symbolism of the Ram.

The equinox had precessed from Taurus into Aries 170 years before the Exodus. Before the Pharaohs there were the Hyksoi, or Shepherd Kings, and before the Hyksoi in Egypt there were the "former writers" on astrology in India referred to by Mihira. This carries us back to close upon 2700 B.C., at which time we find the Hindus already in possession of an astronomy and astrology, to writings upon which Mihira constantly refers.

The Sanskrit kadjan, or palmyra-book, is more ancient than the hieratic papyrus of Egypt. So far as the tile records of Assyria go, they do not approach the antiquity of the Hindu shástras.

Mr. Wilde has laboured to show that the "day for a year" method of directing was in vogue among the Chaldeans, and hence with the Babylonians. This may well be, seeing that Daniel, the chief astrologer at the Court of Nabakollassar (Nebuchadnezzur), declared that, in the first year of the reign of Darius, King over Chaldea, he "*understood by books the number of the years*" of desolation prophesied by Jeremiah, and we find him making use of a period of "70 weeks" to indicate a period of 490 years—*i.e.*, 70 × 7 = 490 days. But if this were the method in vogue among the Chaldeans, it is certain that they were not the preceptors of the Hindus, for, as I have said, the latter have no such time-measure in their astrological books.

4. The insular character of the Hindus, and the exclusive nature of the Brahmin caste, is opposed to the idea of a Chaldean tradition, which could only have been effected by commerce or by means of Mogbeds sojourning in India. In such case the tradition would have left philological landmarks easy of recognition.

That our astrology came to us, from whatever source, by Latin tradition is evident from the names of the signs and planets in use by us. In the same manner, had the Babylonians communicated astrology to the Hindus, the names would have been received by the latter along with the tradition. *Where are the landmarks?* Professor Max Müller takes the contrary view in his famous derivation:

    Deva-pitar = Deo-pitar (Sanskrit).
    Zeus-pater (Greek).
    Deus-pater (Latin).
    Jupiter (English).

There are two names for Jupiter in common use among the Hindus, one (Brihaspati) being the designation of the celestial Father, the other (Guru) being the appellative of the earthly preceptor or "God-Father"

INDIAN ASTROLOGY

—*i.e.*, Deo-pitar. Brihaspati means "Lord of increase," from *Brih* (to expand) and *pati* (Lord). It is identified with the Lord of Creation, Brahma, the latter name having the same root, the Hindu Trimurti or Trinity being Brahma, ♃; Vishnu, ♂; Siva, ♄; literally, the Expander, the Pervader, and the Resolver. They have for consorts Sarasvati, Lakshmi, and Parvati respectively. Hence the unique symbol of the Biune Trinity associated with the seven celestial bodies:

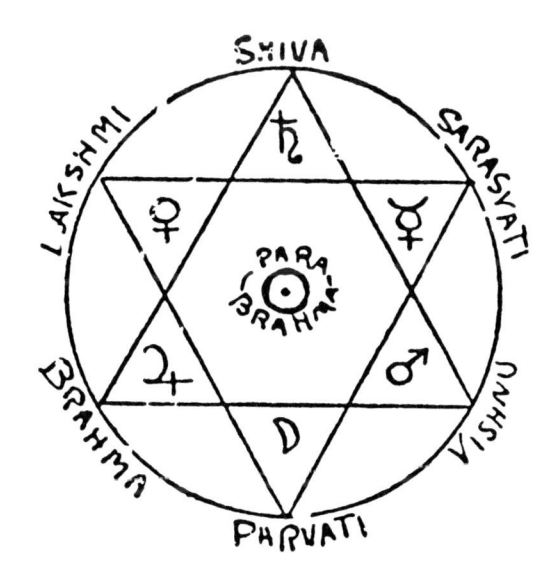

The solar orb in this relation will correspond to Parabrahmam. The male trigon (♄, ♃, ♂) is represented by the right triangle, the female (☽, ☿, ♀) by the reverse triangle, the male and female emanations being opposite in position as in nature; for observe, ♐ and ♓, the signs of ♃, are opposed to ♊ and ♍, the signs of ☿; ♈ and ♏, the signs of ♂, are opposed to ♎ and ♉, the signs of Venus, etc., the opposition being that due to polarity or equilibrium. The twenty-seven asterisms constituting the Hindu zodiac take their names from the principal star in each of them. These stars bear Sanskrit names, not Chaldean.

The astronomy of the Hindus, like their astrology, is original with themselves. The asterisms are subdivided into padams or quarters, each of which is ruled by one of the planets. The periods of the planets are:

Saturn	19 years.
Jupiter	16 ,,
Mars	7 ,,
Sun	6 ,,
Venus	20 ,,
Mercury	17 ,,
Moon	10 ,,
Caput Draconis	18 ,,
Cauda Draconis	7 ,,
Total	120 ,,

The trine is the basis of Hindu astrology.

These details are mentioned in support of the statement that there is *no trace of Chaldean tradition*. The Chaldeans appear to have divided their zodiac into twenty-eight asterisms, and the names of them as received by us are Arabic, showing the channel of tradition.

The insular character of the Hindus, as I have said, is opposed to the idea of a borrowed science. Their terminology is likewise in evidence against the theory of tradition. But what seems to set the matter beyond all doubt is the fact that the Hindus, who are saturated with astrological beliefs, and whose whole life is regulated by these beliefs, present no single monument or structure, no literary quotation, no theological concept, no social law, no single custom which points to such a tradition. Their architecture, on which all inscriptions are in relief, and not in intaglio, as with the Accadians and Egyptians; their ancient language; their classic literature; their theogony; their marriage laws; their methods of life; their regulations in regard to births and deaths—the whole atmosphere of their thought, life, and polity are unique and original with themselves. The religion, science, and language of the Hindus, existing uncorrupted for millenniums, is exclusively and entirely Hindu in its genesis and evolution.

Mr. "A. G. Trent" (Dr. Richard Garnett, LL.D.) says in regard to Hindu astrology: "So far as it differs from European astrology, it appears to differ for the worse. I cannot find any attempt at a theory of Uranus, whose influence is as demonstrable as that of any other planet. At the same time, the small regard paid to the houses seems to me to show that it was not derived from the Arabs, and I am willing to believe it older than Mahomet, while I cannot imagine that it has any such antiquity as the astrology of Egypt or Chaldea."

This is a very important statement coming from so reputable a source, but I venture to suggest another view of the case, which appears to me as more worthy of acceptance. The mere fact that the Hindus have not yet adapted Uranus to their system of astrology (for they are not ignorant of its existence) shows once more the insular reserve of the Brahman, who stands by the Shastras as the meanest individual among them stands by the Dharma (caste) of his progenitors. In India everything is hereditary, inviolate, unalterable. No doubt, in the hands of a European, any difference in the system of astrology taught by us and the Hindus would appear prejudicial to the Hindu system. But put competent Hindu astrologers to the test on their own lines, and I venture to say they will repeat my experience and produce better result with less labour than we by our methods. At the same time I would point out that there are comparatively fewer proficients in India than in Europe. The Hindu astrologers lament the *decline* of Jyotish' shastra, we here regret that the masses have *never even commenced* the study of astrology. In India everyone knows something of it, in Europe the knowledge of it is restricted to a few who are very assiduous in their studies. Astrology is not yet nearly at high noon with us, but it has more than dawned upon those who stand on the hill-tops. In the East they are lying languid in the evening of a resplendent day, and only a few watchers of the night retain a real interest in the glimmering stars.

As to "the small regard paid to the houses," I can only say that every Shastra considers the Bhavas as an essential part of Jyotisha, and a great stress is laid on the several dignities and debilities of the planets in the *houses*, irrespective of the *signs* they occupy. I regret that I have not done justice to this part of the subject in my short exposition of Paràshara in the "New Manual." That Hindu astrology is immeasurably older than the Mohammedan era is certain from the fact that Mihira wrote in the fifth century, at least 120 years before Mahomet, while he makes reference to and quotes from Shastras evidently written 2700 B.C., about 2,200 years before Daniel began the study of the books of prophecy! Narada is regarded by the Hindus as the sage who preserved the ancient astronomical records to those who survived the deluge; and Manu, who struck the keynote of the nation's polity for the Kali Yuja in his famous "Institutes," is held to be one of those sages who bridged over the *ante* and *post* deluvian periods. The "Institutes" of Manu have strict regard to the teachings of astrology, and the conservative Hindu will never neglect the study of his almanac, because the observance of the "Institutes" requires that he should have due regard to times and seasons.

While it is true that we have no evidence to show that Chaldean astrology had its birth in India, it is certainly as true that Hindu astrology cannot be ascribed to a Chaldean source. The horoscopes in the Râmâyana not only enable us to fix the date of that great epic, but also constitute internal evidence of its historical verity. Above all, they prove the great antiquity of Hindu astrology, showing its existence in the peninsula fully 2,000 years before the period ascribed to the Chaldeans. The statement that "the Hindus compute horoscopes incorrectly" is quite false. They calculate the *lagna sphutam*, or rising degree, with great accuracy, and the planets' places are also properly determined in their panchâgamas. But the failings of the Professor must not be laid to the charge of the science, else an equal indictment will dispose of European science forthwith. This I know, the Hindus have records of the influence of every 6' of the zodiac. European astrology has not as yet more than barely delineated the nature and influence of the twelve signs.

As to the many "authorities" who allege that Hindu astrology had its birth in Chaldea, I regret to say I do not know of one Orientalist who has sufficient knowledge of either Hindu or Chaldean astrology to enable him to institute a comparative study. The assertion almost makes one doubt their right to be called philologists or Orientalists. In reference to Dr. Richard Garnett and George Wilde, however, it should be observed that, whereas neither was a reader of Sanskrit, both were competent students and exponents of European modern astrology. Dr. Garnett entertained great suspicions in regard to the antiquity of Aryan literature in distinction from Professor Max Müller, Sir William Jones, and others who were disposed to trace all tradition and language to an Aryan source. Mr. Wilde, on the other hand, had conceived an idea that Chaldea was the birthplace of astronomy and astrology, and even went so far as to call well-known modern methods by the name of Chaldean astrology. Sparse references to astronomical facts to be found in the Accadian and Assyrian records were for him evidences of a complex system of astrology having been current among them. I think it highly probable that such a system existed, but we have no evidence of it, still less that it had the least influence over the astrology of the Hindus.

From my general statement of the Orientalists' position in regard to astrology, it was to be expected that the supposed evidences of a Chaldean or an Egyptian origin of astrology would resolve themselves into a series of unsupported assertions. An authoritative statement can only emanate from one who has made astrology a study. One has only to refer to the star texts of the Bible to see their linguistic study does not suffice for correct interpretation of passages of a technical nature. Reference to an article entitled "The Two Gates," which I contributed to the astrological journal, *Coming Events*, will show the familiar use of the word "gate" as referring to a point of *ingress*. The Book of Judges had received scholarly translation centuries before the gates of Gaza were recognized as the sign Capricorn, or Hebron as the sign Cancer, or yet Samson as the solar body (Shemesh-on), and Delilah as the Moon. In the translation of the Book of Job there are many fancied references to stars where none are intended, and the successional rising of the signs under the name of Mazzaroth has troubled many a commentator.

So in reference to the origin of Hindu astrology, a mere knowledge of Sanskrit does not suffice. The abundant literature of Hindu astrology requires a technical knowledge for its adequate translation. It is true that the Greeks were in a state of rude barbarism while the Egyptians were pursuing an advanced study of astronomy. It is also true that the modern Parsees in India are followers of Zoroaster, but whereas the Hindus have an extensive astronomical literature in the classic Sanskrit, no such record lies to the credit of the Parsees. The statement by the late Mr. George Wilde that "the Indians have some ancient writings of no date" is a very unscholarly remark, more particularly when the tablets of Sargon I. are set in contrast as if bearing an authentic date. The only means we have of judging in the matter is by the internal evidences.

Had the Hindus borrowed their astronomy from Chaldea, or Egypt, or Greece, they would have preserved the landmarks—there would be evidences of tradition. For just as we know that the Saxons were vassals of their Norman conquerors from the contrast of such words as cow (Sax.), beef (Norm.), deer (Sax.), venison (Norm.), sheep (Sax.), mutton (Norm.), etc., and just as we have trace of the Latin tradition in language of our day—as, in fact, we localize the Hebrews and know them to have been a nomadic race from the letters of their alphabet, so we know that the Hindus have no astronomical tradition from Greek or Egyptian. In the naming of the celestial bodies and the asterisms, everything is original, insular, local. Mr Wilde himself advanced a statement which goes far to prove it. "In none of the old Indian writings is any account to be found of the computation of horoscopes by oblique ascension." It has already been shown that the Hindus fix the rising sign and count therefrom, giving to each succeeding sign (*Ras'i*) dominion over a whole house (*Bhava*). Bailly states that "the first tables possessed by the Indians only date back to 3102 B.C." This was the year of the commencement of the Kali Yuga, which opened with the entry of ☉ into the constellation *Mesham* (Aries) in the month of February.

The tables referred to may be the oldest as yet known to us, but it is certain that Varaha Mihira, writing in the year A.D. 498, remarks upon the coincidence of the vernal equinox with the constellation Aries, and of the summer solstice with the constellation (*Katakam*). But in the same passage he states that, "according to former Shastras," the summer solstice once coincided with "the middle of Aslesha" (Leo), and this throws the record back to 3240 B.C. Weber's remark that "it would indeed be a most wonderful play of chance that in all these three countries—Chaldea, China, and India—each in a different spot, but in an identical pole or same latitude, the observations and calculations of the duration of the longest day should be the same," strikes me as being the most puerile thing ever penned by a professed Orientalist. If the countries named are *in the same latitude*, it would only be strange if observations and calculations as to the length of the day at summer solstice should *not* be the same.

Certainly Chaldea, China, and the Aryan country all have common latitude between the Tropic of Cancer and 30° N., and it was in this territory of India that the ancient records were made. A careful survey of the passages quoted by Mr. Wilde reveal no evidence whatever that Hindu astrology had its origin in Chaldea. They do indeed show the antiquity of astronomical records in all the countries named, but there the matter ends, and the evidences of tradition are nil.

THE EVIDENCE OF AUTHORITY

SINCE writing the foregoing defence of Hindu astrology I have had opportunity for a somewhat close study of the work on Sanskrit literature by Arthur A. Macdonell, M.A., Ph.D., and a most absorbing study it has been. I am grateful that my attention was called to the work.

After paying tribute to the labours of his predecessors, including Sir William Jones, Professor Weber, Sir M. Monier-Williams, Professor Max Müller, Professor L. von Schroeder, and others, the author proceeds in the most orderly and graphic manner to set forth the various periods of Indian literary development. A prefatory paragraph of much relevance to the subject of debate deserves quotation: " In writing this ' History of Sanskrit Literature,' I have dwelt more on the life and thought of ancient India, which this literature embodies, than would perhaps have appeared necessary in the case of a European literature. This I have done partly because Sanskrit literature, as representing *an independent civilization* entirely different from that of the West, requires more explanation than most others; and partly because, owing to *the remarkable continuity of Indian culture*, the religious and social institutions of modern India are constantly illustrated by those of the past."

I have set some few words in italics which do not so appear in Professor Macdonell's book in order to bring them under closer observation by the general reader, for they show, in connection with the tenor of the whole work, that the insular character of the Hindu is responsible for the preservation of the Vedic language in almost its pristine purity at the present day. Indeed, this has been my contention from the beginning of the discussion of Hindu astrology in these pages, and I propose to follow Professor Macdonell to his conclusions.

"Among all the ancient literatures," he says, "that of India is, moreover, undoubtedly in intrinsic value and æsthetic merit second only to that of Greece. Its earliest period, *being much older than any product of Greek literature*, presents a more primitive form of belief, and therefore gives a clearer picture of the development of religious ideas than any other literary monument of the world.

"Although it has touched excellence in most of its branches, Sanskrit literature has mainly achieved greatness in religion and philosophy.

"The importance of ancient Indian literature as a whole largely consists in *its originality*. Naturally isolated by its gigantic mountain barrier in the North, the Indian Peninsula has ever since the Aryan invasion formed a *world apart*, over which a unique form of African civilization rapidly spread, and has ever since prevailed. When the Greeks, towards the end of the fourth century B.C., invaded the North-west, the Indians had fully worked out a national culture of their own, *unaffected by foreign influences*. Persians, Greeks, Scythians, and Mohammedans, the development of the life and literature of the Indo-Aryan race remained practically unchecked and unmodified from without down to the era of British occupation.

"No other branch of the Indo-European stock has experienced *an isolated evolution* like this. No other country except China can trace back its language and literature, its religious beliefs and rites, its domestic and social customs, through an *uninterrupted development* of more than three thousand years."

Professor Macdonell gives some striking illustrations of this conservative characteristic of the Aryans. He points out that Sanskrit is still the language of the cultured, spoken as it was centuries before our era. It is still used for literary purposes, and manuscripts are copied, maugre the advantages of printing. The Vedas are learned by heart to-day just as before the invasion of Alexander, and "could even now be restored from the lips of religious teachers if every manuscript or printed copy of them were destroyed." The religion is the same, the social customs remain unaltered. "In various branches of scientific literature, in phonetics, grammar, mathematics, astronomy, medicine, and law, the Indians also achieved notable results. In some of these subjects their attainments are, indeed, far in advance of what was accomplished by the Greeks."

Our attention is riveted by the statement that "history is the one weak spot in Indian literature. It is, in fact, non-existent." Professor Macdonell attributes this feature of Indian literature partly to the fact that as early India made no history it had no occasion to write any, and partly to the doctrine of quietism advocated by the Brahmans, whereby the externals of life became of small interest.

The controversy on the antiquity of the Vedas is of vital interest, but Professor Jacobs grounds his statement that the Vedas are traceable to at least 4000 B.C. on astronomical calculations connected with the change in the beginning of the seasons. But Macdonell thinks the whole estimate to be invalidated by the assumption of a doubtful meaning in a Vedic word which forms the starting-point of the theory. Nevertheless, there is something to be said for this line of argument, as we shall see. "Meanwhile," says our author, "we must rest content with the certainty that Vedic literature, in any case, is of considerably higher antiquity than that of Greece."

Dr. Buhler is cited as authority for the statement that the script of India was of Semitic or Phœnician origin, and dates back to the ninth century B.C. But when it is known that the native learning has always been, and is still, largely traditional and oral, this fact scarcely affects the ground under survey; for, as Macdonell truly says: "The sacred Scriptures, as well as the sciences, can only be acquired from the lips of a teacher, not from a manuscript, and as only memorial knowledge is accounted of value, writing and manuscripts are rarely mentioned."

This peculiar practice of the Aryans shows that the beginnings of Indian poetry and science go back to a time when writing was unknown. The inference is that "writing could have been long in use before it came to be mentioned."

I cannot here follow Professor Macdonell through his fascinating study of the various periods of Indian literature, neither is it essential to the purpose of this review. I will, therefore, pass at once to that part of the work which treats of Western intercourse with the people of Aryavarta.

"The oldest trace of contact between the Indians and the people of the West is to be found in the history of Indian writing, which, as we have already seen, was derived from a Semitic source probably as early as 800 B.C."

It was not until the Greek incursion of the fourth century B.C. that Europe came into permanent relations with the root-stock of the Aryan race. It will be remembered, however, that at this time India had "already fully developed a national culture." Whether this national culture included the astronomical knowledge which has since so thoroughly possessed the Hindu mind it is difficult to determine, but Professor Macdonell is of opinion that "the ancient Indians had but slight, independent knowledge of astronomy." He considers it probable that they derived their early acquaintance with the twenty-eight Moon-stations from the Chaldeans, through their commerce with the Phœnicians.

It is here, in the astrological department of his work, that Professor Macdonell shows unmistakable signs of immature judgment and defective knowledge. The Jyoshis of India have always been of the Brahman caste, priests or Prohitâs, S'âstris or Pundits. It was not until comparatively recent times, by the breaking down of caste observances, that a Vaishya or Chetty had access to the Jyotish S'âstra or astrological science. Indeed, we may safely say that, as all tradition was oral between Guru and Shishya, between teacher and pupil, it was not till the European incursion that tradition of astrology could have reached the common people. The twenty-eight mansions of the Moon were original with the Arabs, as far as we can trace, and the older Sanskrit works are characterized by a division of the zodiac into twenty-seven Moon-stations or Nakshatras. A twenty-eighth asterism (Abhijit) was added for purposes of Pras'na or *horary astrology*, and this seems to point even more distinctly to a later tradition from an Arabian source. The mere existence of Greek cognates in the technical language of Indian astrology does not carry any weight, more particularly when we regard the statement that "the Indians independently advanced astronomical science further than Greeks themselves."

It is said that "the Sanskrit word *uchcha*, 'apex of a planet's orbit,' was borrowed in the form of *Aux* (gen. *Augis*) in Latin translations of Arabic astronomers," and it is stated that in the eighth and ninth centuries (A.D.) the Indians became the teachers of the Arabs in the science of astronomy. The word *uchcha* means "high," and has nothing whatever to do with "the apex of a planet's orbit." It is a term applied to the "exaltation" of a planet Thus, Varaha Mihira in his "Brihat Samhita" gives Tulâm (Libra) as the exaltation (*uchcham*) of Saturn, but Saturn would then be nearly a quadrant from the apex of its orbit. And this brings one to a statement of Professor Macdonell's concerning Varaha Mihira. Treating of the Kavya or poetic treatise of Varaha Mihira, known as the "Brihatsamhitâ," it is said that this work "can without hesitation be assigned to the sixth century."

If I am not mistaken, it was Colebrooke who first called attention to a passage in this work from which its date can be very accurately determined. I have frequently cited this passage which, translated, runs thus:

"The summer solstice is now in the first point of Kâtakam, and the winter solstice in Makaram. But according to former S'âstras, the summer solstice was once in the middle of Aslesha." It is evident that Varaha Mihira is referring the solstitial points to the constellations of *Makaram* (Capricorn) and *Kâtakam* (Cancer), for he, in common with other Indian astrologers, based his system of Jyotisha upon the *Niryana* or natural zodiac.

In the appendix to the work of Professor Macdonell it is said that the astronomer "began his calculations about A.D. 505, and, according to one of his commentators, died in A.D. 587." Presuming his work to have begun at the early age of fifteen years, he would, by this reckoning, have attained the uncommon age of ninety-seven years.

The calculations from the "Suryasiddhanta" made by the author of the "Kalasankalita," point to the epoch K.Y. 3600 as that when the vernal equinox coincided with the first point of Aries, or, in other words, when *Kâtakam* was coincident with the summer solstice and *Makaram* with the winter solstice. Colebrooke has shown, and it is universally conceded, that the *Kali Yuga* began in February, 3102 B.C., so that K.Y. 3600=A.D. 498, which we must take as the approximate date of the "Brihatsamhitâ." This so nearly corresponds to the actual difference of the equinox and the beginning of the Hindu astronomical year at the present day as to leave no doubt that Varaha Mihira lived at the end of the fifth century, when this observation was made.

We are told that "in algebra they (the Indians) attained an eminence far exceeding anything ever achieved by the Greeks."

Summing up these statements concerning the history

of the Hindus as revealed in their classic language, it appears that—

1. They have evolved "an independent civilization" and "a culture of remarkable continuity."

2. "Its literature is much older than any product of Greek literature," and its importance "largely consists in its originality."

3. The earliest contact of the Indians with the West was through a Semitic channel.

4. When the Greeks invaded the North-west, towards the end of the fourth century B.C., "the Indians had already fully worked out a national culture of their own, unaffected by foreign influences," a development which has remained unchecked and unmodified down to the era of the British occupation.

5. The perpetual custom of oral teaching among the Aryans warrants the statement that "the beginning of Indian poetry and science goes back to a time when writing was unknown," and it therefore follows that if the art of writing was of Semitic origin in the ninth century B.C., as stated by Professor Macdonell, the "fully worked out national culture," which was but partially embodied in the "Siddhantas," must have been originally self-evolved and inclusive of astronomical learning, to which neither the Phœnicians, nor Arabs, nor Chaldeans, nor Egyptians contributed; and this learning must have been orally transmitted long before it came to be written.

It is impossible to reconcile "a fully worked out national culture" with the idea that the "Suryasiddhanta" owes anything whatsoever to foreign tradition. Indeed, Professor Macdonell gives us quite sufficient ground for doubting whether the Yavanas were capable of communicating any mathematical or scientific knowledge which was not already in an advanced condition with the Indians centuries before that knowledge was embodied in the works under review in the "History of Sanskrit Literature."

Mr. B. Suryanarain Row is to be commended for

his enthusiastic defence of Hindu traditional knowledge and scientific and literary achievements among the Aryans. But a good deal of unnecessary fire is kindled to consume that most combustible of creations, the straw man. Speaking of the attacks made upon the Hindu sciences by "Orientalists," and notably the assertion that the Hindus borrowed their astronomy from the Chaldeans, Mr. Suryanarain Row reports that a "great Orientalist says that the horoscope of Râma is not given in the 'Râmâyana,'" etc.

Now, it was never put forward that either Dr. Richard Garnett or Mr. George Wilde claimed any status among Orientalists. Dr. Garnett distinctly stated that he availed himself of "a translation of the 'Râmâyana,' but was unsuccessful in finding the horoscope of Râma therein. It was also suggested that his failure herein was due to the voluminous character of the work. Of course, the horoscope is in every copy of the original epic, and is, no doubt, to be found in the translation referred to. One of my correspondents, Mr. N. N. Ghose, Barrister-at-Law, gives the exact quotation—viz., "Bâlakândam," canto xviii., verses 8-10. With this gentleman I am quite in agreement as to the extensive and accessible nature of astrological references in the early Sanskrit literature, and also as regards the great and unexplored wealth of astrological writings to be found in India, in contrast with the absolute dearth of Chaldean records of the same nature. The digest of all the Egyptian knowledge of astronomy and astrology is to be found in the works of Claudius Ptolemy, notably his "Almagest" and "Tetrabiblos"; but this record was made in the second century, and yet is not in any way an advance upon the knowledge current among the Brahmins many centuries before that period.

The Assyrian records at Assurbanipal contain some references to eclipses and other astronomical phenomena, and the Chinese records of the same nature are probably the most complete to be found in any literature. Here and there we find an astrological observation attaching to the astronomical fact, as, for instance, in the Chinese record of the eclipse of September 5, 775 B.C. ("Siao Ya," ix. 4), the text of which conveys this meaning:

"In the tenth Moon, of which the first day is Sin Mao, the Sun was very badly eclipsed. The Moon hid herself even as the Sun was hidden. And the people of the Earth mourned. This lunation foretells suffering (if) the people do not amend their ways. The four kingdoms are evilly disposed, and do not consult their good. The Moon in eclipse is only a common thing, but this eclipse of the Sun is very evil."

Laplace consulted the ancient Chinese records, which go back to the third millennium B.C., in order to determine the obliquity of the ecliptic. As far back as 1110 B.C. the nature and use of the magnetic needle was known and recorded in China, over 2,000 years before it was known in Europe. The Chinese also knew the resolutions of the right-angled triangle five centuries before the fact that the square of the hypotenuse equals the sum of the squares of the perpendicular and base was demonstrated by Pythagoras. Comets were observed and put on record by Chinese astronomers as far back as 2941 B.C. Nothing of this sort has yet been discovered among the Chaldean records. There is, so far as we know, no *system* of astrology or astronomy to be attributed to the Chaldeans. The notion that they were the custodians of a superior knowledge at a time when "all the people of the Earth were of one language" is peculiar to the Semitic record, and it is well known that the Hebrew record is confined to the history of that race, and that their world was comprised in a comparatively small area of the habitable earth. It is commonly observed that when once a theory has been espoused it is the nature of some people to "worry it off the bone," as the saying is; but when, as in the case of the Chaldean "system" of astrology, there is nothing but the bone to begin with, the discussion is not likely to prove of much advantage.

On the other hand, the merits of Hindu astrology, of which there is an extensive exposition, are passed over with a disparaging silence because some wise man of the West has suggested a Chaldean origin. This looks to me like refusing the meat for the sake of holding on to the bone.

There is a great deal more evidence for a common ground of origin for both Chinese and Aryan astrology than for any tradition between the Indian and Chaldean. It is worth noting that the Chinese have employed a sixty-year cycle in common with the Hindus, giving to each successive year in each cycle a distinctive name. But these cycles were apparently for secular use, since both nations in their astronomical treatises make use of an epoch and era. It may be remarked also that the Chinese and Hindus both commenced their era at a point midway between the winter solstice and the vernal equinox.

The Chinese also make use of a constellatory zodiac (Niryana), which, like the Hindus, they divide into twenty-eight asterisms. Their historical classic ("Shu King") gives the positions in reference to the solstice in the period immediately prior to the Deluge, 2348 B.C., from which it appears that the constellation Taurus coincided with the spring (February 6), Leo with the summer solstice, Scorpio with the autumn, and Aquarius with the winter solstice, as quoted by Mihira from former writers. There is every reason to believe that astronomy and astrology took a definite form and became a system of knowledge about the time when the constellations of Taurus, Leo, Scorpio, and Aquarius, called by astrologers "foundation" signs, held the cardinal points of the annual circle. This would be about 2700 B.C.

As to the horoscope of Râma referred to by Dr. Garnett and located by Mr. Ghose, the following pages will speak more definitely.

HOROSCOPE OF RÁMA.

THE following horoscope is taken from the great Indian epic of "Râmâyana," presumed by Orientalists to have been written in its present form about the fourth century B.C., but said to have been an Aryan epic long before the introduction of writing in India, and to have been orally taught and transmitted from the earliest times. The horoscope of Râma affords a most interesting study for the astronomer, and it will be of the highest chronological value to accurately determine the date at which the planets were, by the Indian method of computing, posited in the signs as shown in the figure. Not only have we to calculate the planetary period backward into the dim vistas of the past, but in doing so we have continually to take into account the continual precession of equinoxes down to A.D. 498, when the Hindu and European zodiacs are presumed to have coincided ("Brihat-samhitâ" of Varaha Mihira), and their further precession beyond that epoch.

It should be remembered that every race has its four Yugas or ages, called *Gold, Silver, Copper,* and *Iron* Ages, and known to the Hindus (*vide* "Vishnu-purâna) as *Satya, Treta, Dvapara,* and *Kali* Yugas respectively. This enables us to understand why Râma is referred to the fifth Treta Yuga.

The Aryan race to which the great Râma belongs is the fifth race of humanity, the fourth being the Atlantean, the third the Lemurian. From the positions given in the "Râmâyana" we know that the Sun was in Mesham (Aries constellation), Mars in Makaram (Capricornus), Saturn in Tulâm (Libra), the

Moon in conjunction with Jupiter in Katakam (Cancer), and the Node in Dhanu (Sagittarius). The birth took place when the Moon was in the asterism of Purnavasu, which extends from 80° to 93° 20' from the first point of the zodiac. The Hindu zodiac begins with the constellation Mesham and the asterism of As'wini, each asterism being 13° 20' in extent. The position of the first point of Mesham in relation to the equinox is determined by precession.

We have already seen that the approximate date of the coincidence of the constellation Aries and the equinox was A.D. 498, but as the mean precession is only 1° in seventy-two years it is quite possible that this approximation may be somewhat at fault. It would, however, hardly affect the problem before us. The reader is referred to "Cosmic Symbolism" ("Equalization of Eras") for further light on this point.

Having regard to the positions of the Sun, Mars, Jupiter, and Saturn in the alleged horoscope of Râma, we may proceed to find an approximate date. Mars comes to the same relative geocentric position in regard to the Sun about the same date every seventy-nine years, and Jupiter every twelve years, while Saturn requires a period of thirty years. But as Jupiter's period is not evenly contained in that of Saturn we must double it. Then two periods of Saturn will give just five of Jupiter. Hence we have the values $79 \times 12 \times 5$, or 4,740 years, as the period required to accommodate the four factors employed. Mercury, whose position is given as Mesham (Aries), and Venus, which was in Minam (Pisces), would be included, as would also the Moon, which completes a revolution in twenty-eight days.

The position of the Node, however, is of importance. The difference of the two zodiacs known as Ayanâmsha (increment of motion) is at present about 20° or days, and if this were a modern horoscope we should look for the Node in longitude 260° to 290°—that is, between

♐ 20° and ♑ 10°, in reference to the vernal equinox. The motion of the Node in the zodiac being retrograde, we find it in this position between September, 1862, and September, 1861. But the calculation is further involved by the fact of precession, which in the course of 4,740 years would cause the equinox to pass through more than two whole constellations. It is this factor of precession which complicates the problem.

But if Râma belongs to the fifth Treta Yuga he must have been born before 3102 B.C., for this is the date ascribed to the beginning of the Kali Yuga, and the precession would then amount to about 49°, so that we should find the equinox in about the eleventh of Aquarius, or 49° west of the place it held at the equinox of A.D. 498. In other words, the Sun transits the first point of the Hindu zodiac at the present time on April 10; in A.D. 498 it passed that point about the time of the equinox, March 21, and in 3102 B.C. it passed the same point at the beginning of February. All these observations are pertinent to a just estimate of the date for which Râma's horoscope is drawn.

We know that the Sun was in the first part of Mesham because the Moon was in Purnavasu, which ends in the 4th degree of Katakam, and this constellation was rising when Râma was born. The birth must therefore have been near noon. In the "Râmâyana," Das'aratha, the father of the hero, is made to say: "The Sun's entry in Pushya being now come, the lagna (ascendant) of Katakam in which Râma was born having begun its ascent, the Moon ceased to shine, the Sun was darkened by day, Mars, Jupiter, and other planets converging like a cloud of locusts," etc. This refers to an eclipse of the Sun in the asterism of Pushya, which occupies the constellation Cancer from 3° 20' to 16° 40', and therefore was in the ascendant of Râma's horoscope.

The figure of the heavens is here reproduced in terms of the Hindu zodiac, the symbols being used to indicate *constellations* and not signs:

84 THE SCIENCE OF FOREKNOWLEDGE

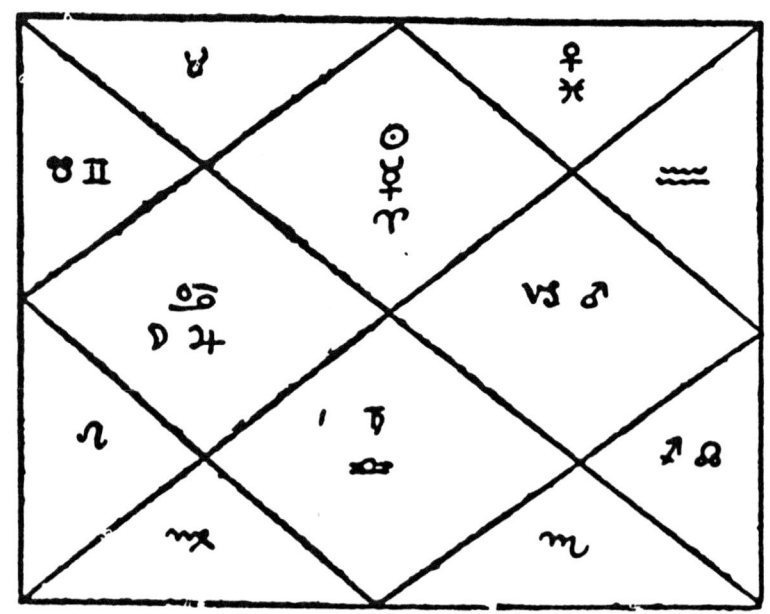

Bentley, in his "Historical View of Hindu Astronomy" (Calcutta, 1823), estimates the birth of Râma from the positions of the planets as April 6, 961 B.C. He uses Lalande's tables for the purpose of computation, and brings out the results as follows:

☉ in ♈	6° 11' 23"
☽ in ♋	12° 13' 54"
♀ in ♓	1° 0' 0"
♂ in ♒	2° 47' 0"
♃ in ♌	6° 24' 13"
♄ in ♎	8° 27' 0"

But Bentley makes a double error in deciding upon this date. He takes the Sayana zodiac, commencing with the vernal equinox, as being that in use with the Hindus, and on this basis brings out an epoch when ♃ is in Leo instead of ♋, and Mars in Aquarius instead of Capricorn.

Having already decided that Râma was born 961 B.C., Bentley discovers that Pushya was not in Cancer at this time, and therefore comes to the amazing conclusion "that the beginning of Cancer and that of Pushya coincided when the author of the 'Râmâyana' wrote this work," and that he therefore concludes, though erroneously, that they were so in the time of Râma.

Hence he deduces that the "Râmâyana" was written in A.D. 295. The fact, however, that the Hindu zodiac began then, as now, with the constellation As'wini, the first point of Mesham (Aries) being coincident with the first of As'wini, shows that Pushya and Cancer (Katakam) coincided then as they do now, Pushya beginning in longitude 93° 20' east of the equinox.

But Bentley confounds himself and his own arguments when he says that the wars of the gods and giants had its origin in the epic of the "Râmâyana," "which fiction, about *two hundred years afterwards, was remodelled and improved by Hesiod and others.*" Herodotus (b. 484 B.C.) places Hesiod and Homer 400 years before his own time—i.e., about 900 B.C. Therefore, according to Bentley, Hesiod, in 900 B.C., borrowed the theme of the war of the gods and giants from the "Râmâyana," which was written in A.D. 295. This is good for a member of the Asiatic Society. Elsewhere I have shown that Professor Macdonell places Varaha Mihira in the sixth century A.D. Bentley requires him near the time of Akbar in the year A.D. 1528. There is no doubt whatever that Professor Macdonell is nearer the truth by *nearly a thousand years!*

I think it reasonable to conclude that the horoscope was calculated by an eminent Jyoshi and introduced as that of Râma. But the question before us is for what date is the horoscope calculated, for that would at all events give us an accurate idea as to the epoch to which the Jyoshi would refer the birth of Râma. One fact, however, is clear from the study of the "Râmâyana." It does not mention the heroes of the Mahábhárata, but the latter has many references to the story of Ráma. Hence there is internal evidence that the "Rámáyana" antedates the epic of the Mahábhárata. The date usually ascribed to the latter is about 600 B.C., and as the story of Ráma could not have been written before Ráma was born, we may conclude that the "Rámáyana" is chronologically located somewhere between the Vedas and the northern epic. The "Rig Veda," the oldest of the Vedas, is supposed to have been compiled about 1400 B.C. There is nothing against the view that the southern epic may not have been traditionally current among the people of the Deccan long before it assumed a literary form under the hand of Valmiki. However that may be, the legend concerns one of the antediluvian heroes who is astrologically referred to the fifth Treta Yuga, which terminated in 3102 B.C. The point of time in question is certainly comprised in the period of 4,740 years prior to the time of Valmiki. The grahasputham of the planets not being indicated, we have no means of making a close calculation, our values being increasingly affected by precession prior to the epoch A.D. 498.

Astrologically considered, there are abundant elements of distinction in the horoscope. Cardinal signs are on angles, and the Sun, Moon, Venus, Jupiter, Saturn, Mars, and Venus are dignified by being in their own or their "exaltation" signs. Thus we have:

☉ in ♈	..	..	..	Exaltation sign.
☽ in ♋	..	..	..	Own ,,
♀ in ♓	..	..	..	Exaltation ,,
♂ in ♑	..	..	..	,, ,,
♃ in ♋	..	..	..	,, ,,
♄ in ♎	..	..	..	,, ,,
☋ in ♐	..	..	..	,, ,,

The Moon, rising in its own sign, has the conjunction of Jupiter and the trine of Venus. A grand cross is formed, by ☉, ♄, ☽, ♂ from cardinal signs and angles. This alone would be adequate astrological indication of fame, apart from other positions of the planets. The horoscope may be purely hypothetical, and it is even possible that the astrologer who is responsible for it may have had no clear idea as to what astronomical date it referred to. Thus it would be possible to place the planets in any given order within the limits of their various geocentric elongations, and assume with perfect certainty that it represents the horoscope of some person born before the year 3102 B.C., but to determine at what date the celestial bodies were thus disposed would impose a task of the greatest magnitude upon even an expert mathematician. All we are able to say is that the horoscope is astrologically in line with the world-wide and enduring fame of the hero of the great Sanskrit epic.

THE ASTROLOGY OF THE HEBREWS

It is not our intention to discuss the merits of the argument that would trace astrology to a Chaldean origin, nor yet seek to determine the relative antiquity of the Chaldeans and the Hebrews. Evidence has been advanced on both sides, showing, on the one hand, that the Chaldeans spoke a dialect of the Hebrew tongue, and, therefore, if they were not themselves of Hebrew origin, they certainly were not—like the Babylonians—the masters of the captive race; while, on the other hand, it has been advanced that the Hebrew was a degenerate offshoot of the more ancient Chaldaic language, one of the arguments being that founded on the fact of the so-called "Hebrew" Scriptures of accredited greater antiquity being written in the Chaldee. Be this as it may, we have the record of the Book of Daniel (partly written in the Chaldean tongue) to the effect that there were sons of Judah at the Court of Nebuchadnezzar, King of Babel, and that they were "ten times" better scribes, magicians, enchanters, and astrologers than the Babylonian Magi, by reason of which Daniel was lifted above them in the favour of the King and honoured with the title of Belteshazzar—i.e., the Prince of Bel. Whatever may be the truth in this matter, it does not immediately concern us, our main object being to show that the Hebrews, from one source or another, were anciently in possession of a system of cosmogony from which they developed a science of astronomy and astrology.

The cosmogenesis of the Hebrews is set forth in the first chapter of *Berasith* (Genesis). The creation of the Sun, Moon, and planets in the firmament was not, as some imagine, a spontaneous production of those bodies from a universal vacuum.

The expansive agitation of the original substance of the heavens and the Earth is conveyed in the word *bra*, a cognate of the Sanskrit root *brih* (meaning to expand), whence we have our word "breathe." The text further says that this *ath heshamayim vath haretz* (elemental condition of the heavens and Earth) was formless (*thaho*) and boundless (*bho*), that there was darkness over the abysm, and that the breath of the *Alhim* (creative powers) fluttered or trembled upon the face of the waters of space. Then came the fiat of the Alhim: "Let there be light!" And there was light. This effective phrase expresses the action of the Alhim (male-female or positive-negative forces) in the primordial substance, typically figured as a boundless and palpitating ocean.

"But how could there be light before the Sun was created?" the superficial sceptic was wont to ask. Science gives the answer when it defines light as *a mode of etheric vibration*. We have our electric light shining through the night, and, so far as mere luminosity is concerned, we are not dependent on the great generator of electrical energy. We know how to store up sunlight during the day, and liberate it through the night hours. So that, after all, the Hebrew idea of the genesis of light does not entail a specific or localized centre of energy. It only requires that the ether of space should be set into a certain mode of activity. This is most scientifically conveyed in the Hebrew word *aur* (cognates *ar*, fire; and *yar*, a river), which means "to flow" or "undulate."

Next came the combination of the elements for the production of fluids and solids, of water and earth, in appropriate centres of space; in effect, a differentiation and specialization of the world-stuff. It is at this point that we came upon the record of Hebrew astronomy. The Alhim made two great lights in the firmament of the heavens to give light to the

Earth, and to divide the day from the night—the greater light for the rule of the day, and the lesser light for the rule of the night, with the planets; and the Alhim said: "Let them be for signs, for seasons, for days, and for years." The true nature and function of the celestial bodies are well defined herein.

They were formed (*óshah*) by accretion of existing elemental matter, the luminosity of the great light-giver being a condition included in the process of its formation. The rule or dominion (*mimeshalah*) of the Sun and Moon over the day and night respectively seems to refer to the influence on mundane things exerted by the rays of those bodies. By the word "signs" (*Otheth*) we must understand indicators or pointers, the word having the root meaning of incipience, beginning, essence. The same word is frequently used to signify a letter or symbol, and also a portent or *augury*. The Sun and Moon, as chronocrators or time-measurers, are familiar from remotest ages, and the significance of the text is quite clear.

That the Hebrews were well acquainted with the divisions of the zodiac (*mazzaroth*) is evident from the prophetic blessing of Jacob, wherein the twelve sons of Israel are, for the first time, associated with their corresponding zodiacal signs. This we may examine more fully at another time. In the Patriarchal days it was customary for the parents of a babe to determine its name from a consideration of its characteristics, genius, or particular destiny, as revealed in the condition of the heavens at the moment of its birth. Thus Jacob himself was named "the supplanter" because he was born with his hand upon the heel of his brother Esau, a circumstance that at once places Esau under ♐ (Sagittarius the hunter) and Jacob under ♑ (Capricornus), for reasons I may state hereafter. In Gen. xxx. 10 we read: *Veyomer Leah: ba-gad. Veyikrá eth shemo Gad.* Zilpah bore Jacob a son, and our text adds, as above, "And Leah said, Gad (Jupiter) is coming up, and they called his name

Gad." This name signifies a troop, a multitude, and is commonly used by the Hebrews as the synonym of good-fortune in the expression, "By Gad!" The same idea is conveyed in the Sanskrit name of Jupiter, *Brihaspati*, "the lord of increase." As the god of Fortune, Jupiter, Gad, Brihaspati, and the Babylonian Baal, or Bel, were names by which the great benefic of astrology was known and worshipped as a power in the heavens.

The ordination of the celestial bodies as rulers or arbiters (Meshâlim) of mundane affairs by day and by night passed as a faith, if not indeed as a traditional knowledge or science, from the Hebrews under the Patriarchs to the Hebrews under the Judges, surviving the foreign influence of the Egyptian captivity through the wisdom of Moses, who, in the institution of the tabernacle, with its "images of things in the heavens," and by means of the Feast of the Passover, preserved the knowledge of astrology to the Levites, and brought the calendar of Israel into agreement with sidereal facts. During their captivity in Egypt the Israelites had been accustomed to witness the worship of the Bull (Apis), in celebration of the New Year, on the Sun's entry into Taurus, a golden disc being placed between the horns of the sacred white bull as a symbol of the astronomical fact. This had continued as a festival among the Egyptians for so long a period that the equinox had passed out of the constellation Taurus into that of Aries without the circumstance having been taken into account, and the worship of the golden calf by the Israelites in the wilderness was an attempt to revive the Egyptian New Year festival. Moses rectified this error by instituting the *Pasach*, or Passover—*i.e.*, the festival of the equinox, when the Sun passed over the equatorial circle. Hence we speak of the *Pascal* full Moon, an astronomical argument used to determine the date of Easter Sunday, and therefore all other movable feasts.

The Hebrews speak of the sheep that is killed at

the Passover as the Pesach; so in 2 Chron. xxx. 18 (âkal pesach): "Eat the Passover." This identifies the month Nisan, the first of the Hebrew calendar, with the zodiacal sign Aries, and shows that Hebrew astrology has been accepted as the basis of the religious festivals of the Christian Church.

Israel, under the Judges, preserved the knowledge of and belief in astrology, and we find evidence of this in the song of Deborah and Barak (Judg. v. 20): *Min-shâmayim nilechamu ı hacocabim om Sisera* ("They fought from the heavens; the planets in their courses fought against Sisera"*). Planetary action is here cited as a causative power in the fortunes of war. The planets in their courses conspired with Israel against the enemy. Napoleon before Moscow, or the Kaiser of Germany in Flanders, might have turned this fact over in his mind had not the genius of an evil destiny blinded him to the fact that he was engaging in an unequal conflict with the powers in the heavens.

In the Psalms of David we have an eloquent expression of the traditional astrology of the Hebrews. Thus (Ps. xix. 1-5) it is said: "The heavens declare the glory of God [Al], and His most precious handiwork the firmament displays. Day unto day seeketh utterance, night unto night showeth wisdom. Without speech and without language their voice is not heard, but in all the earth their rule has gone forth, and their rays to the limits thereof."

The Book of Daniel is replete with astrological allusions, the measure of time adopted in the prophecies being that now current among astrologers—viz., a day for a year; and so also is that of Ezekiel; while in Job xxxviii. 32 we meet with a mention of the zodiac under the name of Mazzaroth: "Canst thou bring forth Mazzaroth [the signs of the zodiac] in their season?" The legend of Samson has been taken by

* The word hacocabim, here rendered planets, is derived from *Cabab*, a hollow globe, not, as often incorrectly stated, from *coal*, to burn.

THE ASTROLOGY OF THE HEBREWS

scholars, such as Drummond and others, to be simply a solar allegory intended to convey a knowledge of astronomical facts under a parable. Such, indeed, it would seem to be, seeing that "Samson" itself means the solar orb, and "Delilah" goddess of the night. In this connection the betrayal of Samson by Delilah would indicate a solar eclipse, the rays of the Sun being "shorn off" by the Moon. The reader will remember that the hair of Apollo was likened to the rays of the day-star. The Philistines (turners or revolvers) come, under this interpretation, to signify the degrees of the zodiac, while Gaza and Hebron are the solstitial signs Capricorn and Cancer.

The Hebrews called the signs of the zodiac "gates," placing "three to the south-east" (Aries, Taurus, and Gemini), "three to the south-west" (Cancer, Leo, and Virgo), "three to the north-west" (Libra, Scorpio, and Sagittarius), and "three to the north-east" (Capricornus, Aquarius, and Pisces), as shown in the subjoined diagram.

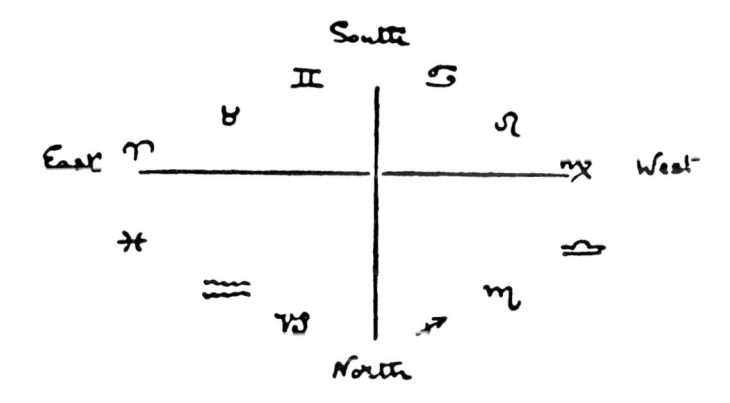

The twelve gates are again mentioned in the Apocalypse, together with the stones appropriate to the twelve tribes of Israel, which, it will be remembered, entered into the construction of the breastplate of the

94   THE SCIENCE OF FOREKNOWLEDGE

High-Priest. These twelve stones are variously given by interpreters, but there is no doubt they were directly associated with the twelve signs of the zodiac, as the seven lights were with the seven celestial bodies—Saturn, Jupiter, Mars, Sun, Venus, Mercury, and Moon.

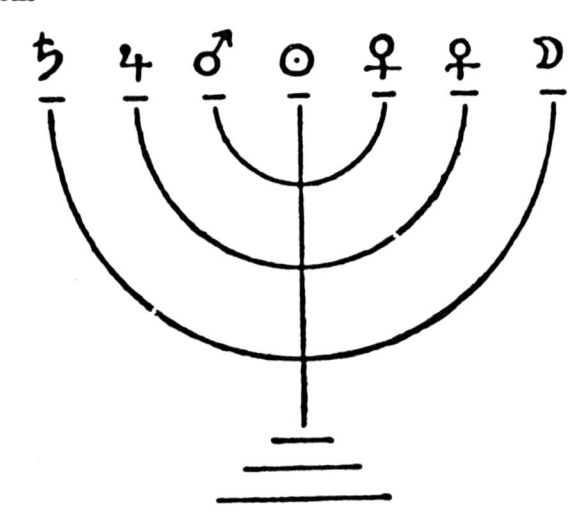

♄ ♃ ♂ ☉ ♀ ☿ ☽

The seven lights on the altar represented the "seven spirits before the throne of God." It will be seen that they are paired or linked together according to their astrological relations thus:

    ♄ opposed to the ☽ as ♑ is to ♋.
    ♃   "   "   ☿ as ♐ and ♓ to ♊ and ♍.
    ♂   "   "   ♀ as ♉ to ♏ and ♎ to ♈.

the Sun residing centrally as king of the solar system in the sign ♌, a god among the planets and their satellites. Hence the name of the archangel ascribed to the Sun—Michael, Mi-ca-el, "who is like God."

The planets, among all peoples, from Mongolians in the far East to the Mexican aborigines in the West, gave their names to the days of the week. The circumstance has been commented upon by scholars as evidence of an underlying identity and original unity among the nations. The Aryans have the same days as ourselves—a Sun-day and a Moon-day, etc., in the same order, and each day is the Sabbath of its presiding deity. The Hebrew's Sabbath is that of Saturn, for the tribes of Israel were the seed of Jacob, whose sign was Capricornus, and whose ruling planet was Saturn, as we shall see anon. The astrological characteristics of the days of the week are conveyed to us in the *Sepher Berasith*, or Book of Genesis. The Hebrews divided their day primarily into two parts—"the evening" from noon to midnight, and "the morning" from midnight to noon.

- ☉ Yom Achad, the first day, was Sunday.
- ☽ Yom Sheni, the second day, was Monday.
- ♂ Yom Shelishi, the third day, was Tuesday.
- ☿ Yom Rebioi, the fourth day, was Wednesday.
- ♃ Yom Hemishi, the fifth day, was Thursday.
- ♃ Yom Hashishi, the sixth day, was Friday.
- ♄ Yom Shebioi, the seventh day, was Saturday.

"And God rested from His labours."

NOTE.—*Achad* is the equivalent of the word On, from which we derive one, only, unit, union, etc. Originally it means a *sphere* or *circle*, hence our word onion, denoting a bulb composed of a series of spheres, one within the other. The circle stands for the symbol of the Sun or Sol, Solis, Sole = the one only.

Sheni means a second or a witness and has special reference to the female principle in nature, which, like the lunar orb, is rightly called: "Un secondo sole dentro breviata sfera" (A second Sun within a shortened sphere).

Adam embodied the solar force, Eve the lunar power. The other days of the Creation are, in the Hebrew, equally suggestive of the dominant characteristics of the planets severally related to them.

The days being thus apportioned to the different planets, the Hebrews further divided them into hours, counting sunrise as the sixth hour, terminating at noon in the day and at midnight in the night. The first hour was governed by the planet which gave its name to the day, and was followed by the other planets in their order, thus

```
                              SUNDAY.
       A.M.: 1   2   3   4   5   6   7   8   9   10  11  12
   Sunrise→ ☉   ♀   ☿   ☽   ♄   ♃   ♂   ☉   ♀   ☿   ☽   ♄
            ☿   ♀   ☉   ♂   ♃   ♄   ☽   ☿   ♀   ☉   ♂   ♃  ←Sunset
            12  11  10  9   8   7   6   5   4   3   2   1 P.M.
                              MONDAY.
            1   2
   Sunrise→ ☽   ♄ , etc.
```

The Hebrews believed that each planet had a tutelary deity or spirit, and if we suppose the planets to be inhabited, like the Earth, with humanities suited to their several stages of evolution, it is reasonable to regard the "planetary spirit" as the co-ordinating centre of consciousness, representing the mass chord of spiritual activity in the planet's humanity. The spirits presiding over the several planets were thus named:

>   The Sun ruled by Michael.
>   The Moon ,,   ,, Gabriel.
>   Mars   ,,   ,, Samael.
>   Mercury ,,   ,, Raphael.
>   Jupiter   ,,   ,, Zadkiel.
>   Venus   ,,   ,, Haniel.
>   Saturn   ,,   ,, Jophiel (Casial).

By these names we understand the Incomparable, the Deific, the Powerful, the Wrathful, the Healing, the Just, the Glorious, and Mysterious. The Egyptian equivalents are: Ra, Neit, Khem, Nauph, Ammon, Mut, and Sat.

We have already seen that the signs of the zodiac (Mazzaroth) were well known to the Hebrews, and the allotting of these signs to the twelve tribes of Israel, together with the destiny thence arising, is set forth in (Gen. xlix.) the prophetic blessing of Jacob.

To *Reuben*, the first-born, was given the first sign of the zodiac, Taurus. The more earthly characteristics of Venus are depicted in the reference to his

THE ASTROLOGY OF THE HEBREWS

unlawful intercourse with Bilhah, his father's concubine. Some astrologers, being led astray by the epithet "unstable as water," have placed this tribe under the sign Aquarius, forgetting that Aquarius is not a watery sign, but an ethereal one, the highest of the airy trigon. The key to this matter lies in the fact that Jacob and Esau were a twin. Esau was a hunter (Sagittarius), while Jacob (the supplanter) was the following sign Capricornus. Hence, as we have said, he was ruled by Saturn. Now Taurus is the fifth sign from Capricornus, and properly represents the first-born of Jacob. Moreover, the first letter of the Hebrew alphabet is taken from the first sign of the zodiac—viz., Aleph (a bull), i.e., Taurus. The word *Aleph* means a chief, principal, head, leader, etc., in agreement with the characteristics of the first constellation of the Hebrew zodiac.

"*Simeon* and *Levi* are a twin." The sign ♊, with its adjunct Cancer, are here specifically mentioned. "Instruments of cruelty are in their hands," we read, and this at once calls to mind the city of London (ruled by ♊), with its patrons, "Gog and Magog," who still retain the *Cali hamas* (instruments of cruelty). Simeon means one who proclaims, or declares; the nature of ♊ and its planet ☿ (Mercury) being thus portrayed. Levi means "joined to." The Dioscuri (Castor and Pollux) are identified with the constellation of the Gemini. The Levites were the sacred or sacerdotal tribe, the picked men among them being chosen for the priesthood. Simeon and Levi led the assault against the people of Shechem, whom they murdered. For this, they received their father's curse, and became scattered among the tribes. We learn that, on account of the narrow limits of their inheritance, many of them (Simeonites and Levites) became scribes, while on account of their curse they were commonly despised among the tribes.

"*Judah*, thou art he whom thy brethren shall praise," as the name imports. "Thy hand shall be upon the neck of thine enemies" recalls the well-known monument of the lion setting his paw upon the snake's head—a type of the Lion of the tribe of Judah overcoming Death. Judah as Leo is further localized in the heavens by the statement: "The sceptre shall not depart from Judah, nor the lawgiver from between his feet, until Shiloh shall arise; and unto him shall the gathering of the people be." The arising of Shiloh has reference to the star in Scorpio, which goes by the name of Shulah, at the rising of which star Leo drops from the meridian, together with Cepheus and his sceptre. Reference to the celestial globe will make this fact apparent to the reader. It is worthy of remark that the Royal Arms of England comprise *Leo* (the lion), *Sagittarius* (the unicorn), the country itself being under the dominion of the martial sign *Aries*, thus embracing the complete fiery trigon ♈, ♌, ♐.

Zebulon is Virgo, "the haven of ships," the name coming from the root *Zebel*, a haven. They had their coast or limits "near to Sidonia," as the text says, for their possessions lay between the Sea of Galilee and the Mediterranean. They were great fishers, and enriched themselves by their commerce. In the region of the constellation Virgo will be found that of the Argos, or ship. Hence the saying, "A haven for ships."

Issachar is described as "an ass bending between two burdens" and "a servant of tribute." These are the characteristics of the sign Libra, the balance, a beam between two scales, a symbol of justice. The Judge Tola may be mentioned as the most notable of this inconspicuous tribe. The name comes from Telah, to weigh; and is the equivalent to the Sanskrit Tulâ, the name of the sign Libra, the balance. Hence we may derive such measures of quantity as a *toll*, a *tale*, a *till*, a *tally*, etc.

"*Dan* shall judge his people as one of the tribes of Israel." Dan means knowledge, or wisdom, and is

used to signify judgment, hence the name Daniel—
"A Daniel come to judgment!" Jordan, which
separates the wilderness from the Holy Land, gets its
name from *Yar*, a river, and *Dan*, knowledge; and it
symbolizes the state of vastation or purgatory between
this world and the next.

"Dan is a snake in the way, a serpent in the path,
that biteth the horse-heels, so that the rider falleth
backward." This is a parallel of the prophecy concerning the serpent and Adam, of whom it is said,
"Thou [Adam] shall bruise his head, but he [the
serpent] shall bruise thy heel," and is preserved to us
in emblem by the figure of St. George and the Dragon
on the standard coin of the realm. The scorpion,
serpent, dragon, snake, hydra, and eagle, are all
related to this constellation Scorpionis, and will be
found in juxtaposition on the celestial globe. The
serpent is sometimes used as denoting wisdom, sometimes deception, and also both life and death. The
name Dan, a judge, is a cognate of the Hindî word
Dána, to know. The Danites of Laish were noted for
their dark knowledge.

In the *Evening News* of March 22, 1900, the following
statements were made:

"Monday, April 23, will be the feast of St. George,
patron of England. English soldiers deserve a national
tribute, and April 23 is the day to pay it. For St.
George is a soldier-saint. He was an officer in the
Roman Army, and lost his land in the persecution of
Diocletian, about A.D. 303. The Order of the Garter
is founded in his honour, and so late as 1614 it was the
custom to wear blue coats on St. George's Day in
imitation of the blue mantle of the Garter. In old
days England fought under the banner of St. George;
and, according to Shakespeare, Henry V. led the
attack on Harfleur to the battle-cry of 'God for
Harry, England, and St. George!' By a glorious
coincidence St. George's Day is also the anniversary
of the birth and death of Shakespeare."

100 THE SCIENCE OF FOREKNOWLEDGE

Without desiring to unnecessarily disturb the historical associations referred to in the above extracts, we would remark that St. George is one of the ancient Masonic landmarks of the calendar, and is derived from *Geo-urgon*, from the entry of the solar orb into Taurus, the agricultural sign represented by the ox. We all know the legend of "St. George and the Dragon," and of "Bel and the Dragon." Bel, or Baal, is the solar orb. The word means "strong," and is cognate with the Sanskrit *Bali* of the same meaning. The bull or ox is a symbol of strength, and in the Hebrew the word Aleph (bull) is the name of the first letter of the alphabet—the sign ♉ being the first of the Hebrew and Egyptian zodiacs—and is synonymous with the words "chief," "leader," "foremost," "highest." The word *Alp* signifies a high place, and is the name given to a mountain. Hercules is also a symbol of strength, and his conflict with the hydra is a parallel of that of St. George with the dragon, for both these represent the solar influence in Taurus in conflict with the opposing sign-influence of Draco, Serpentarius, Scorpio.

The statement that the feast of St. George coincides with the birth and death anniversary of Shakespeare is a calendaric error. St. George is identified with April 23, it is true, but Shakespeare's birth took place on a day which corresponds to May 4, the solar equivalent for April 23 (O.S.). The coincidence, therefore, only arises from the fallacious system of putting " new wine into old bottles "—a practice every astronomical student must beware of.

"*Gad*" may mean a troop or good-fortune. In the original there is a peculiar play upon the root word thus: *Gad gadud igudenu vehwa yaged áqeb*. This reiteration of the word signifying a troop of horsemen emphasizes the identity of the tribe with the sign Sagittarius, the armed horseman, ruled by the planet Jupiter, the star of good-fortune, or Gad.

Asher means blessed. " Out of Asher the oil of

his food [shall come]; and he shall yield the fare of a king." The dignities of the sign Capricornus as the chief of the earthly trigon are here set forth. The term *modnimelech*, translated "royal dainties" or "kingly fare," should, in our opinion, be rendered the "pleasant things of Melech"—*i.e.*, of the planet Saturn, which was known as Melech. The Israelites were forbidden to make offerings to Melech, and a curse was put upon those who passed their seed "through the fire unto Melech." It does not refer to the sacrifice of their children to an idol, as some suppose, but to secret vice. The word Melech means a king.

"*Naphtali* is a hind let loose; he giveth goodly words." The Septuagint version is far preferable: "Naphtali is a spreading tree (*ailah shelchah*), yielding leafy branches (*imri-sapher*)." The tree is a symbol of the human race, and the Messiah, or God-man, is spoken of as the Tree of Life, "the leaves of which are for the healing of the nations." The saints, "men made perfect," are called "trees of righteousness." The man restored to vision saw men first of all "as trees, walking." From these considerations we can see the identity of Aquarius with the tribe of Naphtali, the spreading tree. Reference to the primitive root *Otz* will throw some further light on this subject.

"*Joseph* [*lit.*, He shall gather] is the branch of a vine, of a fruitful vine by a pool, whose branches run over the wall." Drummond, in his "Œdipus Judaicus," affirms that the text, "*oli-din benuth*," has reference to the hen and chickens upon the back of the ass, "*oli-shur*"; and so, indeed, it may, since it has the evidence of the ancient planisphere in support of it. The Babylonians represented the *Succoth-Benuth* in the region of their zodiac to which this tribe is referred—viz., Pisces—the position being that of the constellation, not of the sign so designated. Dagon, the man-fish, was worshipped by the Philistines as the deity of *increase,* whence some philologists derive the name from Dagan—*i.e.,* corn—and it is singular that Joseph's remarkable storage of corn was the means of his exaltation at the Egyptian Court.

Joseph was the progenitor of the "Shepherd, the head-stone of Israel," and was called in Egypt Zaphnathpaneah—*i.e.,* Saviour of the world. Joshua, the antetype of Jesus—the names are identical in the Hebrew tongue—was "the son of Nun"—*i.e.,* of the fish—and the word Ishvâ (Joshua, or Jesus) means "He shall save," and the Saviour made His disciples "fishers [saviours] of men." The fruitfulness of the sign Pisces is astrologically determined beyond all doubt, and the identity of the tribe of Joseph with that sign is well supported by the singular blessings promised to Joseph—blessings of the heavens above and of the Earth beneath, blessings of the breast and of the womb, etc. The sign of Pisces is ruled by Jupiter.

"*Benjamin* shall raven as a wolf. In the morning he shall devour the prey, and in the evening he shall divide the spoil." Benjamin means son of the right hand. Judah (Ω) was the lawgiver. Gad ($\f$) was the "right hand of the law"—*i.e.,* the fifth constellation from Ω—and Benjamin (Υ) is the "son of the right hand"—*i.e.,* the fifth constellation from $\f$. He is depicted as a ravening wolf, improvident, attacking at first and depleting the fold, and afterwards, by a transformation of character, sharing all the spiritual plunder. Paul was a good example of the Benjaminite.

In the beginning and the end of the Jewish dispensation they were remarkable for their valour and conquests. They were famous warriors, and very skilful in the use of weapons. These are the characteristics of Marsmen. The Egyptian planisphere represents the constellation Aries by a man with the head of a wolf: Anubis (the awakener). This is the same as the *Aishcaleb,* or man-wolf, of the Hebrew Kabalah, and the Æsculapius (the healer) of the Greeks.

THE ASTROLOGY OF THE HEBREWS

The dream of Joseph is synthetic of this distribution of the signs among the tribes, for the " Sun, Moon, and eleven stars " that make obeisance to him were Jacob (his father), Rachel (his mother), and his eleven brothers. To this day the Sun is astrologically the significator of the father and the Moon of the mother.

It may be as well to repeat, in this place, that there is no warrant for the " sweet influences of the Pleiades " so often quoted from Job xxxviii. 31: *Hatheqesher modenuth kimah ao-moshecoth kesil tipetech* (" Canst thou bind the tremblings of heat, or loose the cold seal ?"). This *kesil* is the cold influence of month November-December, which is named *Kislu*. In Brown's " Dictionary of the Bible " we read that the Pleiades " appear at the end of March," being in the neck of Taurus. Hence he speaks of the fresh winds and warmth which attend their rise. As a matter of fact, they " appear " in autumn and winter, not in the spring and summer. The sweet influences of the Pleiades, as every astrologer knows, are a minus quantity.

THE STAR OF BETHLEHEM

For many generations prior to the beginning of the Christian era there was current in the East a tradition which promised the advent of a Messiah, one who should rule the world as a King of Kings, and who should be born of the tribe of Judah.

Isaiah, the Prophet, in the eighth century, B.C., and Micah, about the same time, had specifically predicted the birth of such a ruler. Thus Mic. v. 2: " But thou, Bethlehem Ephrata, although thou art the least of the heads of Judah, from thee shall go forth He who shall rule in Israel, and whose goings forth are from of old, from times eternal." The text seems to convey the idea that these " goings forth," or manifestations of the godhead in the flesh, had previously occurred at different times from the most remote ages of the world's history. One is impelled to recall the mysterious figure of Melchisedek (King of Righteousness), who, " without father and without mother, having neither beginning of days nor end of life," yet walked the earth " in the similitude of the Son of God," and talked with Abraham.

In the same way the prophet Malachi led the Hebrews to expect a reappearance of the Prophet Elijah (Elias), and this belief in the periodic manifestations of Deity and in the reincarnation of souls is conspicuous to all who read Scripture in the light of truth and for truth's sake.

At the period when the narrative of the Nativity commences, 4 B.C., a Messiah was daily and hourly expected by the Jews, and the expectation had doubtless extended to the Armenians, Arabs, Chaldeans, and possibly the Persians, all of whom had intimate commercial and general relations with the Syrians.

Renan makes this expectancy the mainspring of what he considers to have been an ambitious but misguided evangel. In fine, he would have it that, but for the fevered anticipation of the people, there had been no Messiah whatsoever. He makes the carpenter's son the mere by-product of a popular ferment, a bubble that swelled in the midst of the froth, exploded—*et voilà, tout!* But then we may say we did not expect a Renan. So why did he intrude? *Ex nihilo nihil fit.* Certainly not a Christendom.

However, as we have seen, a Messiah was expected, and the Scriptures say that a Messiah was born, according to prophecy, in Bethlehem of Judea, about six miles south of Jerusalem. In the last year of Herod the Great, 4 B.C, Augustus Cæsar commanded a registration of the Jews in Palestine. Accordingly, every family repaired to its tribal division, and Joseph, with his wife Mary, journeyed from Nazareth to Bethlehem (the birthplace of David) " because they were of the house of David." On their arrival at the inn they found it fully occupied by those who had come a shorter distance, or had travelled quicker than they. They took refuge in the adjoining stable. There Jesus was born.

Simultaneously, there appeared in Jerusalem certain Magi from the East inquiring for the new-born King of the Jews, saying they " had seen His star in the east, and were come to worship Him." Naturally, an announcement of that kind, coming freshly from the lips of strangers who had travelled from afar—men whose distinctive office was sufficient to secure them a respectful audience—would cause something more than a flutter of excitement. As a matter of fact, " Herod was troubled when he heard it, and all the people with him." But Herod's health was failing, and he had no son to succeed him. What were the priests and scribes doing, that they had no knowledge of this great event? Let them come to Herod and declare where the Christ should be born! They had but one source of inspiration—the Prophet Micah—and they quoted him: "In Bethlehem of Judea." And they were right. Jealous of this new-born King, Herod despatched the Magi to Bethlehem, persuading them with cunning words to return and report to him.

It is here that we come upon the vagaries of that bright particular star, popularly known as the *Star of Bethlehem*. The Magi had seen it in the east—we are not told how long since. Now, as they travel southward from Jerusalem, the star appears to move before them, reaching the meridian just as they approach the inn of Bethlehem. "And they saw the star and rejoiced exceedingly." They found the Child lying in a manger.

What was this star, and how did it guide the Magi to the birthplace? These questions we may examine in the light of astrology.

The Magi had seen His star in the east; then why did they go *westward* to Judea? We reply: When they say they had seen His star "in the east," they did not mean in the eastern horizon (the geographical east), but in the east of the zodiac, in the region of the constellation Aries. They knew it was the portent of a kingly birth, because they were astrologers, and argued rightly from the importance of the phenomenon. They determined the place to be Judea, because Aries was the ruling sign of that country. Knowing so much, they did not wait for more, but made their preparations for the journey to the Jewish capital. As this expedition, whether proceeding from Chaldea or Persia, would occupy many days, the "star" must have appeared some time before the birth, and probably it increased in brilliance until the event.

Treating the star as a real celestial phenomenon, though of an extraordinary and special order, it is probable that the object appeared in the beginning of the sign Aries, with a declination of about 32° N., which is the latitude of Bethlehem (*circa* 31° 40' N.).

Further, it is necessary to observe that the obliquity of the ecliptic was then 23° 44', about 16' more than now. It should, moreover, be noted that the first point of the constellation Aries was then about 7° in advance of the vernal equinox. It is now about 20° behind the equinoctial point. The Chaldeans and Hebrews reckoned by the constellations or lunar mansions, and not from the equinox, as did the Greeks, whose system we have adopted.

As to the month in which the Nativity took place, we must regretfully consign the popular idea to the region of myth, and for no other reason than that of climate. We are told that "there were in the fields shepherds, keeping watch over their flocks by night."

The latitude of Bethlehem (31° 40'), taken in relation to the sun's extreme south declination (23° 44') on the December 25,* shows that its rays, even at high noon, would have an obliquity of 55° 24' in regard to Bethlehem, and this angle corresponds to the middle of March in our latitude, 51° 28' N. If anyone who can get the loan of a sheep or two cares to try watching over flocks by night during the middle of March anywhere in these latitudes, he will get a true idea of the popular carol which represents the shepherds "all seated on the ground" at midnight on the December 25! It is this particular incident of the shepherds "watching by night" that specially helps us to fix the probable month of the Nativity as either August or September, the hot season of Palestine. We may choose August, for the following reasons:

1. The period between the Nativity and the death of Herod the Great was ninety-four days. Now, as the Tetrarch died in the same year that Jesus was born, 4 B.C., and near the end of November, the Nativity must have taken place in August.

* This and the following days were formerly the Saturnalia of pagan Rome.

108 THE SCIENCE OF FOREKNOWLEDGE

2. The registration or census of the Jews under Cæsar would no doubt have been fixed for the commencement of the Jewish civil year, in the month *Tishri*, which in the year began on September 6. The mandate of Cæsar would have regard to the ordinances of the Jewish law. Joseph and Mary always went up to Jerusalem to keep the Passover, and probably it was also their custom to attend the Feast of Tabernacles, which took place on the 15th of Tishri—that being one of the seven great occasions of Jewish celebration. Hence there would be convenient reason for the Mother to be in or near Jerusalem towards the end of August.

3. If we count ninety-four days prior to November 25, on which day Herod died, we come to August 23, according to Archbishop Usher's calculation. On this day the sun enters the zodiacal sign "Virgo," the virgin, and the thirteenth lunar mansion *Altaire*. What more befitting the virgin-born King than this entry of the solar orb into the sign which, in all countries, was held to typify the Immaculate Mother?

As to the exact hour of birth, there is nothing in the text which serves to guide us to a true estimate, but we know that the Nativity had taken place when the star "stood over the house where the Child lay." We can reasonably assume that the star must have held a prominent position in the horoscope of the great event, and as we have determined its position in the beginning of Aries, we may safely consider that part of the zodiac to have been just in the east at the moment of birth.

In support of this idea, the following reasons are adduced:

1. If the Magi arrived in Jerusalem just about the time of the birth, or before it had risen, it is evident why they could not point to it in witness of their words, "We have seen His star." Later on, when they had had audience of Herod and had learned from an assembly of the priests and scribes that Bethlehem

was to be the birthplace of the King of the Jews, they set out on their journey thither, and they "saw the star" (now high in the heavens) and rejoiced.

2. The first asterism or lunar mansion corresponding to the first 13° of the sign Aries is called *Al Natha*, "the slain lamb." Throughout the Scriptures the lamb (ail), or Aries, is a type of the Messiah. The Crucifixion took place about the time of the Passover, in the month of April, when the Sun was in the sign Aries.

3. A calculation shows the planet Mars to have occupied the zodiacal sign Leo at the Nativity. Mars, as the god of war, fitly determines the significance of the words, "I came not to bring peace, but a sword," and here we find the ruddy planet ruling Aries, the natal sign, and posited in "its own lion," in conjunction with Neptune and Mercury. However, Jesus was spoken of as "the Lion of the tribe of Judah," that tribe being under the sign Leo, as in Gen. xlix., "Judah is a lion, an old lion crouching down," etc. Hence Jesus was a Lion of Lions, a King of Kings, and rightly portrayed by the regal, solar sign Leo.

4. A further calculation shows Saturn to have been rising in the sign Aries, afflicting Venus in Cancer by a malefic square aspect, and the full Moon in the sign Pisces occupying the House of Sorrows (twelfth) in opposition to the Sun in the House of Suffering, and approaching a conjunction with the malefic planet Uranus. Two texts immediately spring into memory: "A Man of Sorrows and acquainted with grief," spoken of the Messiah by the prophet; and "My kingdom is not of this world," spoken by the Man of Sorrows of Himself.

In conclusion, I have approached this inquiry in the light of Scripture and the light of reason, and I find them not incompatible. It is worthy of comment that a brilliant star, far outshining Venus in lustre, was observed by Tycho in the sixteenth century, and the same star was seen in the thirteenth and tenth centuries.

It occupied a position above the head of Andromeda, about 82° N. declination, and from its first appearance gradually increased in splendour till it could be seen in the daytime, and then waned and finally disappeared. In the year 4 B.C., Andromeda's longitude was coincident with the beginning of the sign Aries, and therefore with the Star of Bethlehem.

JOAN OF ARC

In his Foreword to the translation of the ancient French manuscripts of Jean François Alden in the archives of France, Mark Twain says:

"The details of the life of Jean of Arc form a biography which is unique among the world's biographies in one respect. *It is the only story of a human life which comes to us under oath, the only one which comes to us from the witness-stand.* The official records of the Great Trial of 1431 and of the Process of Rehabilitation of a quarter of a century later are still preserved in the National Archives of France, and they furnish with remarkable fulness the facts of her life. The history of no other life of that remote time is known with either the certainty or the comprehensiveness that attaches to hers."

From this statement it will be seen that the following facts, taken verbatim from Mark Twain's work, may be relied upon as authentic: Jeanne d'Arc was born at Domremy, in lat. 48° 27′ N. and long. 5° 40′ E., on January 6, 1412. Corroborative evidence is contained in the work already cited, the opening words of which read as follows: " I, the Sieur Louis de Conte, was born in Neufchâteau on January 6, 1410—that is to say, *exactly* two years before Joan of Arc was born in Domremy."

This Louis de Conte, it should be said, was the page and secretary of Jeanne d'Arc during the wars, and her companion in childhood. The family to which Joan belonged was composed of Jacques d'Arc, the father, Isabel Romée, the mother, and their issue—viz.:

Jacque, born in 1406;
Pierre, born in 1408;
Jean, born in 1409;
Joan, born in 1412; and
Catherine, born in 1415.

The d'Arcs led a pastoral life, and Joan was accustomed to tend sheep and cattle. From the first dawn of intelligence Joan gave evidence of a remarkably gentle disposition, a high moral perception, a precocious intellect, and an extraordinary sense of justice. As a girl she evinced great moral courage, and from the age of thirteen years she was the subject of a series of remarkable visions which she discreetly kept to herself. It was not until May 15, 1428, that Louis de Conte, her companion, was a witness of these visions. But on that day the secret of her singular life was revealed to him in a vision of the angel Michael, which appeared to her at the same time. Hereafter he was her confidant in all these spiritual experiences, and the rest of his long years were devoted to her service and to the record of her daily life.

It was on January 5. 1429, the eve of her seventeenth birthday, that Joan gave substance and point to her continual assertion that she was advised to save France. "The time has come," she said. "My voices are not vague now, but clear, and they have told me what to do. In two months I shall be with the Dauphin."

This statement, seemingly so presumptuous from the mouth of an obscure maiden, was literally fulfilled, and her peculiar spiritual perception was singularly confirmed by a ruse which the King thought to play off upon her. The Court being assembled, Joan was ushered into the presence of the Dauphin. When presented to him who sat in the royal seat, Joan regarded him steadfastly, making no obeisance, and presently turned and went towards a group of courtiers; then, seeing one among them whom she knew to be the King, she fell on her knees at his feet and delivered her message of salvation for France.

Undecided how to act with regard to Joan, though strongly disposed in her favour, the King—a victim of jealousy and mistrust in addition to a naturally weak character—referred her to the Bishops. Their verdict, after many days of careful scrutiny and examination of the Maid, was delivered as follows: "It is found and hereby declared that Joan of Arc, called the Maid, is a good Christian and a good Catholic; that there is nothing in her person or her words contrary to the Faith; and that the King may and ought to accept the succour she offers; for to repel it would be to offend the Holy Spirit and render him unworthy of the aid of God."

Upon this verdict the King's edict was made: "Know all men and take heed therefore that the most high and illustrious Charles, by the grace of God King of France, hath been pleased to confer upon his well-beloved servant Joan of Arc, called the Maid, the title, enrolments, authorities, and dignity of General-in-Chief of the armies of France, and hath appointed to be her Lieutenant and Chief of Staff a Prince of the Royal House, His Grace the Duc d'Alençon."

Think of it! Only two months before, this maid was a simple peasant without any other hope of recognition than that which is the common fate of untutored genius. To-day she is General of the armies of France! Can we say otherwise than that God did it? Did it by the appointed ministers of His will, the stars of heaven—revealed it by the mouth of His angel.

It is unnecessary to recount the onward march of that triumphant army over whose destinies this simple maiden exercised so strange and magical an influence.

It was at Orleans, on May 8, 1429, that the maiden wrought her genius at its highest pitch. After a seven month's beleaguerment, "a thing which the first

Generals of France had called impossible was accomplished by her in four days." Orleans was taken! In this assault Joan was struck between the neck and shoulder by an iron bolt from an arbalest. Thereafter she was known as the Maid of Orleans, but the common name for her was "La Pucelle."

Restoration to power turned the King's head. Victory upon victory perverted his sense of duty. So much glory was ascribed to him by the sycophants of the Court that, in a sense, he came to believe that he had earned it for himself, or that it was his divine right. Then, acting upon evil counsel, he began to tamper and hinder the Maid by his egotistic meddling as much as by his weakness and vacillation. The end came, as it was bound to come sooner or later, by this policy of vanity and weakness.

The Maid was taken prisoner by the English and delivered by treaty into the hands of the clergy, who arraigned her on an accusation of infidelity to the Church. For three long months she was daily subjected to cross-examination by the most astute minds that France could muster. She stood before them in irons just as she had come from her prison cell. They heckled her at all points every day for hours together. She never faltered, never uttered a compromising word, never swerved from the simple truth as she had spoken it to the King at Rouen two years before. But she showed the spirit of the true soldier, and frequently, too, the tactics of a true General. She was unconquered by these learned minds, and confounded them by her own simplicity of faith.

But the King's weakness undid her. During all that unholy inquisition, which had but one object—the degradation and death of the saviour of France—the King never once sent a word of encouragement, nor even stretched forth a finger to help the Maid. He sold her to the English, and they sold her to the priests. The trial extended from February 21 to May 24, 1431, and on that date she was taken to the stake and publicly condemned to perpetual imprisonment. She had been ill with low fever and in terrible bodily pain since March 29. On May 30 she was again taken to the stake, and in the presence of all those whom with her own blood she had released from the yoke of years, the Maid suffered the death of the martyr. Not since Calvary can history produce any act more infamous, black, and diabolical than this persecution of La Pucelle; not since the Man of Sorrows was any life more worthy to be called divine. Charles had his crown and kingdom, and Joan—she had hers.

In considering this beautiful and tragic history from the point of view of the astrological science we have first to remember that all the dates mentioned are in old style, and that their equivalents are eight days later in the new style. I have been at some pains to calculate the places of the planets at the birth and death of Joan of Arc, and here set them out for the information of the student.

The solar decan of the martial sign Scorpio is rising, Mars, its ruler, being in the tenth house in the Mercurial sign Virgo. The Moon is in conjunction with the violent and martial star *Regulus*, in the meridian of the horoscope. This position of the lunar orb in the regal sign Leo gave her that claim to the recognition of royalty and the nobility of France which eventually brought about her tragic end. Neptune in the eighth house shows treachery and conspiracy against her life. Saturn, in the western angle, is an evidence of the persistent enmity directed against her, and also, being in mutual disposition with Venus, the ruler of the seventh house, it indicates that inherent sanctity and purity of life which captivated and subdued the roistering soldiery under her command. Her age at death was 19 years 4¼ months, affording an arc of 19° 22'. The Moon, by its position in the figure, holds the prerogative of hyleg, and by an arc of 19¼° Mars came by direction to conjunction with the Moon.

116 THE SCIENCE OF FOREKNOWLEDGE

PLANETS' PLACES AT BIRTH, JANUARY 6, 1412, NOON
(DOMREMY).

☉ ♑ 24° 13'; ☽, ♌ 24° 21'; ♅, ♋ 8° 46'; ♄, ♉ 17° 4';
♆, ♏ 5° 30'; ♃, ♎ 14° 1'; ♂, ♍ 13° 51'; ♀, ♑ 17° 2; ☿, ♐ 29° '.

PLANETS' PLACES AT DEATH, MAY 30, 1431, NOON
(DOMREMY).

☉, ♊ 15 38'; ☽, ♑ 2° 25'; ♅, ♋ 10 33'; ♆, ♈ 26° 33';
♄, ♑ 24° 28'; ♃, ♉ 28° 22'; ♂, ♎ 19° 43'.

The luminaries and superior planets only are given.

No record is made, so far as I am aware, of the hour of birth, and in considering this matter, I was strongly tempted to regard *Virgo* as the rising sign on account of the singularity of the names given to Jeanne d'Arc, "The Maid" and "La Pucelle" (the Virgin). This would have given a rising position to Mars, but for astrological reasons I was forced to abandon it.

Joan, or Jeanne, is a name which belongs, like the English John, Johanna, etc., to the sign Scorpio, and Orleans is ruled by that sign also. It will not, therefore, be surprising to the student who is a continual witness of these "coincidences" of astral signature to learn that the rising of the sign Scorpio in this horoscope of the Maid of Orleans satisfies all the requirements of her singular life and character.

	♎ 22°	♍ 26°	♌ 24°	♋ 15°	♊ 9°
♏ 10° 47'	♂ 14° 1'	♀ 13° 51' ☽ 24° 18' Regulus		♅ 8° 46'	17° 4' ♄
	♃ 29° 0	♀ 17° 2 ☉ 24° 13' ♆ 5° 30'			10° 47' ♉
	♐ 9°	♑ 15°	♒ 24°	♓ 26°	♈ 22°

In short, I find that she was born under the 11th degree of the sign Scorpio, with Mars, the ruler of the Nativity, in the sign Virgo. I may at once present the figure of the heavens at the birth, leaving the student to consider it in the light of astrological evidence. I find that at the time of death, at 19 years 4 months, the ascendant was directed to the semisquare of Mars in the zodiac. The mid-heaven was directed to a conjunction with Mars in the zodiac direct, and to the opposition of Uranus in zodiac converse. By comparing the places of the planets at death with those of the Nativity, it will be seen that Saturn was upon the place of the Sun, while Uranus was just past the quadrature. By secondary direction the Moon was in ♉ 11°, and therefore in opposition to the ascendant. At the commencement of the trial the Moon was square Uranus.

THE MEASURE OF LIFE

AMONG a number of researches into the laws governing the time of birth, it was my good-fortune to happen upon a series of coincidences which seemed to foreshadow the existence of a law. The investigation was made with the object of finding the time of birth when only the day was known. It seemed plausible that the date of birth was in some intimate manner connected with the date of death—that the extremes of life held a certain definite relationship to one another, which, when regarded as an arc of the circle of existence, should be capable of more or less exact measurement.

Further, it is already known that by the measure of time employed in astrology—viz., one day after birth for each year of life—a certain day after birth (known as the progress) will correspond to the year of death, just as the day of birth itself corresponds to the year of birth. Hence the general proposition: As the progress is to the birth, so is death to x. This x will be a certain other date constituting the fourth term in the proportion. If we call the day of birth B, the progress P, and the day of death D, it will facilitate explanation.

In solving the proportion, as $P : B :: D : x$, it will be necessary to use a common denomination; and in measuring the arc B, P, corresponding to the age of a person, it will be found convenient to state it in terms of right ascension or sidereal time. Having thus found the values of B, P, D, and x, in a series of cases, I discovered that the determination of the radical mid-heaven followed from one of six resolutions—viz.:

THE MEASURE OF LIFE

1. $B+P+x$.
2. $B+P-x$.
3. $B-P+x$.
4. $B-P-x$.
5. $P-B-x$.
6. $P-B+x$.

A few illustrations will suffice to show the method of this calculation by which it is proposed to determine the *horoscope of birth* from a knowledge of the date of death alone; and, conversely, to determine the *date of death* from a known horoscope.

EXAMPLES.

LORD TENNYSON, born August 6, died October 6.
Age at death, 83 years.
Progress = October 28.
As $P:B::D:x$.

		h.	m.	a.c.
Oct. 28.—Sidereal time	..	14	29	8·90550
Aug. 6.— ,, ,,	..	8	58	1·30264
Oct. 6.— ,, ,,	..	12	59	1·14189
x ,, ,,	..	8	2	1·350003
Add B		8	58	
		17	0	
Subtract from P		14	29	
Remains		21	29	M.C. at birth.

This is so nearly the radical M.C. in right ascension as to be remarkable. The poet himself stated his birth hour to be "just after midnight." The equation is of the sixth order.

Shelley, the poet, is known to have been born under the twenty-sixth degree of Sagittarius, with R.A. of M.C. 13h. 59m., the equation being $(B-x)+P$, the second order.

Byron was born under Cancer, the equation being of the third order, $(B+x)-P$.

E. A. Poe was born under ♏ (Scorpio), the third equation, $(B+x)-P$.

Shakespeare was born under Virgo, the equation being the converse of the fifth order, $P-(B-x)$.

Sir Isaac Newton was born under Libra, the equation being the same as above.

President Garfield was born under Virgo, the equation being the converse of the second order, $P+(B-x)$.

Dante was born under Gemini, the equation being the converse of the first order.

The fact that we have an alternative of six different equations shows that something yet remains to be done. We must know by some means which of the equations to take, and further research will no doubt reveal a definite rule.

I have stated the ideas as they occurred to me, and have adduced a few of the many cases which seem to support the general proposition. There are many ingenious students of astrological laws who will no doubt have both inclination and opportunity to extend the research while I am occupied with other problems. I would point out, before leaving the subject in their hands, that, when once the equation is determined, the application of it to any fatal year will determine the day of death. The following is additional data in support of the general theorem of this measure:

R. G. F., male, born March 12, 1854, 8.30 a.m., Norwich; died October 31, 1893. Taurus rising. Resolution $=P-(B+x)$.

S. T. Coleridge, born October 21, 1772, 11 a.m.; died July 25, 1834. Sagittarius rising. Resolution $=P-(B+x)$.

W. E. Gladstone, born December 29, 1809, 8.18 a.m., Liverpool; died May 19, 1898. Capricorn rising. Resolution $=(P-B)+x$.

E. M. W., female, born February 23, 1888; died October 15. Scorpio rising. Resolution $=P-(B+x)$.

A number of anomalous cases are gradually accumulating, and will no doubt form a most valuable means towards a more perfect definition of the law after which we are seeking. So far as research goes, the large majority of cases fall well within the terms of the general theorem.

Mr. H. S. Green has very aptly digested this theorem of the measure of life in the following words:

"There is some necessary relation existing between the right ascension of the Sun and that of the mid-heaven at birth" (*Coming Events*, vol. v., p. 170).

"Birth implies death, and the conditions and date of birth imply the conditions and date of death" (p. 169).

Bearing these passages in mind, it will be seen, on reflection, that the necessity of relationship between the radical Sun and mid-heaven means nothing more or less than a necessity of birth-time, which, regarded as an incident in the chain of causation, is an adjunct of the doctrine of pre-established harmony—a doctrine that is only questioned by those who regard the established harmony of the universe as the result of "a fortuitous concurrence of atoms."

Accepting the doctrine as fundamental to a rational concept of astrology, we see that the birth-time is a thing fixed and determined—necessitous. There is a necessary relation of the Sun to the meridian, as of the new-born individual to the local conditions of life.

The theorem goes farther than this. It argues a necessary and definite (though as yet undetermined) relation between the day and the year; between the Sun's advance in the zodiac after birth and the advance of a person in years; between the progress of the Sun in the zodiac and the revolution of the Earth on its axis; and, finally, between the date of death and the date and hour of birth.

I may cite an example elsewhere mentioned—that of the birth and death of Queen Victoria. The theorem of the measure of life is expressed in the proportion:

As $P : B :: D : x$.
P = Progress, Aug. 13, 1819 = 9h. 28m.
B = Birth, May 24, 1819 = 4h. 9m.
D = Death, Jan. 22, 1901 = 20h. 5m.
Then x = 9h. 24m.

On reference to the ephemeris it will be found that this value of x, in terms of sidereal time, corresponds to August 12.

1. This date is *one day*, or 0h. 4m., *short of the progress*.

2. The Sun on January 22, 1901 was in ♎ 2°, and this is 1° (day), or 0h. 4m., short of the *radical mid-heaven* (♎ 8°).

This observation is most significant and suggestive. One point that is brought into prominence is the fact that, astrologically, or perhaps I should say *astronomically*, the day is 24h. and 4m., which is equivalent to saying that, astrologically, the "year" is 1 day and 4 minutes in length. Therefore the Queen would, astrologically, attain her eighty-first birthday just eighty-one days after May 24. This date is already known as the progressive birthday. The mid-heaven and the Sun advance 1° for each year of life, always retaining the same relations to one another as at birth (taken in terms of right ascension).

Now, if we add 81° to the long. of the mid-heaven in the Queen's horoscope (♎ 2° 24′+81°) we obtain ♈ 28° 24′ as the progressed position. This corresponds to April 13, and from January 22 (the fatal day) to April 13 = 81 days. Had the Queen died on any other day of the year the exact correspondence would not have been maintained.

Thus we see by what an array of eloquent evidence the science of astrology is sustained, even in the study of a single horoscope. It is an elevating and inspiring thought that the upbuilding and welding together of the Empire, the enfranchisement and material welfare of its people, and the thousand lasting benefits to which our children are heirs, all are consequent upon the accession of a gifted and good Queen to the British Throne—not a circumstance of chance, but the provident design of an All-wise Deity whose will is written eternally in the heavens.

Akin to this theorem is that of the tidal analogue, which I have discovered to be connected closely with the moment of birth, and possibly of use in determining that too often problematical time. I take the following from the pages of the *British Journal of Astrology*:

"There may be a necessary relation between the luminaries at the exact moment of a birth. The fact that the universe is conformable to recognized laws of motion would certainly uphold the suggestion of such a relationship of birth to the incident of luni-solar action. What is there, for instance, underlying the following calculation of the prime factors in relation to the horoscope of King George V.?

"The sun was in Gemini 12° 16', its distance from the nearest equinox being 72° 16', or 4h. 49m. 4s. The Moon was in Libra 1° 4', and distant from equinox also 1° 4', or 0h. 4m. 16s. The distance between the Sun and Moon was three signs 18° 48', or 108° 48', half of which is 54° 24', this being the point representing tidal action, or 3h. 37m. 36s. from both luminaries.

	h.	m.	s.	
Then	4	49	4	Sun from equinox.
Less	3	37	36	Tidal point.
	1	11	28	
Plus		4	13	Moon from equinox.
	1	15	44	
Plus	12	0	0	hours to midnight.
Equation		2	0	
	13	17	44	= 1h. 17m. 44s. a.m.

The recorded time of birth was 1h. 18m. a.m.

"Another instance, showing a variation of the same factors, may be cited:

	h.	m.	s.
Sun in Pisces 29° 43', distant from equinox	0	1	8
Moon in Leo 22° 43', distant from equinox	2	33	8
Half-distance between Sun and Moon	4	46	0
The difference of these latter factors is	2	12	52
From which subtract sun from equinox	0	1	8
Result	2	11	44
Or	26	11	44
Hours to midnight and equation, less	12	2	0
	14	9	44
Or a.m.	2	9	44

Recorded time of birth, 2.10 a.m.

"The case from Right Hon. Lloyd George's horoscope works as follows:

	h.	m.	s.
Sun in Capricorn 26° 53', distant from equinox	4	12	28
Moon in Sagittarius 24° 35', distant from equinox	5	38	20
	9	50	48
Half-distance Sun-Moon = tidal point	1	4	36
	8	46	12
W. long. and equation	0	12	2
	8	58	14

Certified time of birth, 8.57 a.m.

"A case well known and tested from data, January 29, 1864, at 3.10 p.m., London, affords another variant from the same factors as the above. Thus:

	h.	m.	s.
Half-distance between ☉ and ☽	3	54	44
Less ☉ from equinox	3	23	56
Difference	0	30	48
☽ from equinox	0	46	36
☉ from equinox	3	23	56
Difference	2	37	20
As above	0	30	48
	3	8	8
Equation			31
p.m.	3	8	39

The family record is 3.10 p.m., or rather over a minute later.

"It becomes an interesting question, from the evidence supplied by these and many other cases which have come under my observation, as to whether the births of individuals do not take place in conformity with a tidal law which is everywhere apparent in the world about us, and which doubtless has its extension in some manner, as yet but partially defined.

in all sublunary phenomena. The ancients regarded the Sun as symbolical of the paternal, and the Moon of the maternal functions in the natural world, and the employment of these two factors in their combined action upon the earth would doubtless lead to many useful conclusions if scientifically examined. In astronomy there are two equations for determining the Moon's position in its orbit, which have been handed down from Ptolemy and Tycho (both capable astrologers), and which are called respectively the evection and variation. The formulæ for these are: Evection $1° 16' \sin. 2 (MS) - A$, and variation $40' \sin. 2 (M-S)$, where A equals the anomaly. Substituting the distance from the equinoctial point (east or west, as the case may be) for the distance from Aphelion, the examples before us offer distinct mathematical analogy to these equations. There is an old salt-water saying that dying men 'go out with the tide.' It is also probable that they *come in with the tide*, and those who have studied my thesis of the prenatal epoch will be in a position to appreciate this suggestion."

ASTROLOGICAL PRACTICE

UNDER this title we may now consider the more technical and practical side of our subject. Admitting for purposes of study that the radical positions of the planets, both as to sign and the quarter of the heavens in which a planet and sign may be at the moment of birth, have a signification, if not an influence, in regard to the person, it has been a matter of special study to determine the different periods of life at which the indications of the horoscope may be expected to have fulfilment. This process is called "directing." Fundamentally it consists in bringing the body of our planet to the position held by another at the moment of birth.

Primary directions are those made by the motion of the luminaries, the mid-heaven and ascendant (called significators), whereby they form aspects to the places of the planets (called promittors), and similarly the motion of the planets, whereby they form aspects to the radical Sun, Moon, mid-heaven, and ascendant. There are various methods in vogue among astrologers, but all have the same end in view, and the measure of time is always one day or one degree=one year of life.

Secondary directions are formed by the Moon's diurnal motion in the zodiac after birth, accounting one day as a year, whereby it forms aspects to the places of the planets in the radical and also to those places they have severally attained by direction.

PTOLEMY'S METHOD

Ptolemy, in his "Tetrabiblos" (A.D. 130), shows us how to calculate the arcs of direction by bringing a succeedant planet in the zodiac to the position of a precedent one, as seen from the place of birth. A planet in Aries is precedent to one in Taurus, and one in Taurus is succeedant to one in Aries. If a planet is on the mid-heaven at birth, another is brought to it by right ascension, the intervening degrees being the arc of direction. But if a planet is on the ascendant or east horizon, another that is below it is brought to the same place by degrees of oblique ascension, and the arc will then be the number of degrees which pass over the mid-heaven during the ascent of the succeedant planet to the horizon. The oblique ascension is determined by the latitude of the locality and the declination of the planet.

But when a planet is neither on the mid-heaven nor nadir, and neither on the ascendant nor descendant of the horoscope, then it will have a position answering to a latitude or locality which is proportionate to its distance from the mid-heaven and horizon. For there is no ascensional difference due to the mid-heaven, and that due to the ascendant is determined by the latitude of the place of birth. We must therefore take the proportional distance of the planet from the mid-heaven and refer it to the whole arc described by the planet from its rising to its culmination; or from its setting to its transit of the nadir, according as it may be above or below the horizon; or from its meridian to its horizontal passage, as the case may be—which measure is called the semi-arc, being half of its passage above or below the Earth. It is determined by the declination of the body and the latitude of the place. Thus we obtain a pole or latitude between 0° and the latitude of the place of birth. Then the oblique ascension or descension of the body under that pole, and the oblique ascension or descension of a succeedant body under the same pole, will differ by the arc of right ascension which is required to bring the one planet to the place of the precedent planet, as seen from the place of birth.

This constitutes the whole method of Claudius

Ptolemy, and it has had advocates and exponents in all climes ever since it was formulated by the great astronomer. I have called it a method advisedly, for it does not present the co-ordinated results of a system. Each factor has to be dealt with separately, and in the process the integrity of the radical horoscope is left out of sight. There can be little doubt that the method affords some valuable pointers, but it will be seen that there is no uniformity of motion among the several factors, and the labour involved is very considerable. A co-ordinated and easy method of dealing with the primary arcs will be found in my " Primary Directions made Easy," which enables the student to bring out arcs of direction to within three months of the exact time by mere reference to a Table of Ascensions or Table of Houses.

In distinction from the highly mathematical method of Ptolemy and its extension by Placidus de Titus, we have the Arabian system commonly in vogue among Western astrologers. This consists in merely setting a figure of the heavens for each successive day after birth at the same time as the birth, accounting each day as a year of life. The natural geocentric motions of the planets in the zodiac are thus brought into account, and the aspects formed by them to the radical places of the significators are noted. Simultaneously the progress of the mid-heaven, ascendant, and Sun are observed, and their aspects to the radical positions taken into account. These form the *primary* indications. The *secondary* indications are formed by the Moon's apparent motion in the zodiac during each day after birth, and the aspects thus formed by it to the radical and progressed positions are noted, together with the sign and house in which the planet in aspect to the moon may be at the time. Each day after birth being equal to one year, every two hours of the Moon's motion is equal to one month, and thus we get mensual indications which are entirely absent from the Ptolemaic method.

The system here briefly defined has been variously

applied and amended by different writers, but the principle remains the same, and is that most commonly subscribed to by students. As a variant of the scheme I may here cite:

BONATTIS' METHOD OF DIRECTING.

In the "Universa Astrosophia Naturalis" of Antonio Francis de Bonattis, printed in Patavia, 1617, the following system of natural astrology is explained and illustrated:

The natural motion of the heavens and of the heavenly bodies, as observed in relation to the Earth, or any part of it, is taken as the ground-plan of the system. The Earth, by its diurnal rotation on its axis from west to east, causes the celestial concave to assume an apparent motion in the opposite direction. By this apparent motion the planets rise, come to the meridian, and set, forming aspects in *mundo* to the mid-heaven, ascendant, and their opposite angles. The space traversed by the meridian from one conjunction with the ☉ to the next is the increment of one year's direction. It is neither one degree of right ascension nor one degree of longitude, but the difference of the Sun's longitude from day to day, following upon that of birth. In effect, a figure is cast for each day after birth, applying the hour of birth to the sidereal time at noon on each day succeedant to the birth.

So far, the idea is not remarkable for its novelty, having been previously applied by Julius Firmicus and Placidus de Titus. It will be observed, however, that the Sun becomes the true chronocrator or time-maker by its diurnal motion, which at certain seasons is *less*, and at certain others *more*, than one degree a day. The operation, in short, is nothing more or less than the direct direction of the meridian in the zodiac, and that of the ascendant under the pole of the birth-place; for with each direction of the M.C. a new ascendant is taken out under the latitude of birth from the Tables of Houses, or otherwise, as may be the more agreeable.

When, however, we come to consider the planetary positions in the directional horoscope thus obtained, we find Bonattis contending for a new and a more natural order of things. In the system of Firmicus (*Placidus delucidate, non invente*) the Sun, Moon, and planets retain their radical longitudes, which by this motion of the heavens are brought successively to aspects and conjunctions with the angles and one another. Bonattis, however, contends against this as being contrary to nature, for he argues from the fact that at such time as the meridian shall be increased by a certain right ascension, the Sun, Moon, and planets will not be found in their radical places, but each body, according to its natural motion in the zodiac of the Earth, will have increased or diminished its longitude according to whether it be direct or retrograde. He therefore takes out the true longitude of the planets for each succeeding day, and applies them to the progressive horoscope for these days, and in this particular he makes no exception of the Moon. The mundane and zodiacal aspects and parallels are then apparent from a mere inspection of the figure.

The work by Bonattis is illustrated by numerous horoscopical figures bearing out this system, and others in which the progressive revolution is put forward on the same grounds. The system strikes one as being natural, and therefore probably true.

Of the virtue of transits over the progressed midheaven, ascendant, Sun, and Moon, we have had ample and striking proof in a variety of instances, and in these pages we have repeatedly called attention to it. The progressive places of the significators are therefore capable of actual affection by the coincidence of transits, lunations and eclipses, and it is not unreasonable to suppose, from that circumstance, that they are equally susceptible, as significators, when directed as Bonattis recommends.

But to bring matters to the test of true or false is a matter as easy as it is essential.

To commence with our own experience, the death of the father may be taken as the first great event of life, happening as it did at the age of 4 years 1 month and 10 days. Correcting the time of birth from this event by the direction of Asc. ☍ ♅ m. con.—

Semi-arc ♅	55° 52'
Merid. dist. ♅	51° 46'
Asc. ☍ ♅	4° 6' = 4yrs. 1m. 10d.

—there remains the fact that ♃ came to the M.C. at one of the direst and most troublous periods of the life—viz., at 26° 42' as measured by its meridian distance. By the system of Bonattis, however, ♃ being retrograde in the horoscope, its meridian position is attained in the twenty-sixth year. Thus, 25 days after birth, the Sun is in ♈ 24° 47', and at birth in ♓ 29° 43'; difference = 25° 4'. Radical M.C. ♏ 0° 50' + 25° 4' = ♏ 25° 54'. The radical position of ♃ is ♏ 27° 31', ℞ and the progressive place 25 days after birth is ♏ 26° 2', so that it attained its meridian position at 25 years 2 months, which actually corresponds to one of the most prosperous periods of the life. Arc of direction: M.C. ☌ ♃ = 25° 11'.

Probably a consideration of this circumstance of the natural motions of the planets would account for the futile attempts to read astrology into the horoscope of the late Queen Victoria, which hitherto has baffled and perplexed the advocates of Placidus. In this instance, the progressive position of ♃ at 18 days after birth is brought to the meridian by an arc of 18° 5', exactly as required by the event of Her Majesty's accession to the throne; and this without in any way encroaching upon the traditional time of Her Majesty's birth, which is stated by Simmonite as 4h. 4m. 35s. a.m. It will be observed that ♃ attains the required longitude 18 days after birth, and presently turns retrograde, thus allowing the formation of the exact arc of direction M.C. ☌ ♃ 18° 5'.

We recommend the system of Bonattis of the student as worthy of close investigation.

THE RADIX SYSTEM

Having opened up the subject of "directions" by a brief summary of the methods generally in use among experimental students and public exponents, I am now in a position to lay the foundations of a more complete and at the same time facile method of my own discovery. The main features of any consistent measure of time must, in my belief, show all calculations to be directly related to the radical horoscope—*i.e.*, the horoscope for the moment of birth—and the indications derived from calculation must be in terms of that radix. If, therefore, we assume that the Sun, Moon, and planets maintain their radical relations throughout the life of an individual, and at the same time affirm that the subsequent aspects formed by them, either by direction of the significators or by that of the planets themselves, are to be taken as pointers or indications from which prognostics can be formed, there can be only one method and one measure of time. For it is obvious that a degree of right ascension is not equivalent to a degree of the zodiac, nor either of them to one day. One day of 24 hours is one revolution of the Earth on its axis *plus* 4 minutes, because during 24 hours the Sun advances 1 degree in the zodiac. Hence 360 equatorial degrees are not equal to 24 hours, but to 23h. 56m. Thus, if the meridian of a place were in line with the Sun in Pisces 15° at noon, one rotation of the Earth would bring it again to that point of the zodiac, but it would require another 4 minutes of time to bring it into line with the Sun, now in Pisces 16°.

Moreover, we cannot say that 1 degree of the zodiac

equals 1 year, since there are 365 days in the year and 360 degrees in the zodiac. Hence the mean increment of the Sun is not 1 degree, but 59' 8" only. Hence we may argue that the longitudinal increment of 59' 8" is the measure for one year.

Next as to the method. No system which does not maintain the radical relations of the planets can lay claim to integrity or consistency. For it is above all things certain that the radical imprint of the heavens is that from which the argument is derived as to tendency, aptitude, opportunity, and circumstance in the character and life of an individual, we may thereafter direct Jupiter to the mid-heaven, or the ascendant, or to the good aspect of the Sun or Moon; but the detached significance of the planet cannot be rightly judged apart from a consideration of its radical relations and affections, and this is the chief cause of expectancy being disappointed in many cases. Similarly, Saturn may be in radical benefic relations with other planets or with the luminaries, and its direction to a significator would bring that significator into simultaneous benefic relations in the zodiac with these planets or luminaries, and thus Saturn's direction would be shorn of its malefic indication by its conjunction with the significator, and some loss of an aged relative might be attended by advancement and material benefit, as is usually the case. Obviously an afflicted planet cannot indicate any substantial benefits even from its most benefic directions to the significators. Nor can a planet that is radically well aspected indicate by malefic direction any serious hurt, for with its direction to the conjunction or opposition it will simultaneously bring up the sextiles and trines by which it was attended at birth. Failure to take these points into consideration has led to many errors of judgment in the estimate of probable results, and any system which depends for its prognostics upon the detached indications of the planets may be regarded as incoherent and inarticulate.

184 THE SCIENCE OF FOREKNOWLEDGE

The following method is therefore advanced as the most consistent and fully-tried system as yet published, and has been in use for some time by the author, with the very best results:

The SIGNIFICATORS are the Sun, Moon, Mid-heaven, Ascendant, and Part of Fortune. The mid-heaven is fixed by the addition of time, plus equation at 10 seconds per hour, to the sidereal time at noon on the day of birth. The ascendant is taken out by Tables of Oblique Ascension (or Tables of Houses) due to the latitude of birth under the right ascension of the mid-heaven. The places of the Sun and Moon are taken from the ephemeris for the year of birth.

Part of Fortune, otherwise called FORTUNA, is found by subtracting the longitude of the Sun from that of the Moon, and adding the result to the longitude of the ascendant. This gives a zodiacal position as far removed from the ascendant as the Moon is from the Sun.

Example.—The Sun being in Pisces 29° 43′, and the Moon in Leo 22° 43′, the ascendant in Sagittarius 24° 43′, we have the following calculation for the place of Fortuna:

Moon's longitude	.. ..	4ˢ 22°	43′
Sun's longitude.	.. ..	11ˢ 29°	43′
		4ˢ 23°	0′
Ascendant longitude ..	..	8ˢ 24°	43′
		1ˢ 19°	43′

Which is equivalent to Taurus 19° 43′, in which we place the symbol.

The planets' places are also taken out for the time of birth from the ephemeris and placed in the figure under their proper symbols. The horoscope is now complete, and the system of direction from this horoscope for any given period of life requires no further reference to the ephemeris.

DIRECTION is made by adding to the mid-heaven an

arc equivalent to the age of an individual at any epoch. We then have the longitude of the directional mid-heaven for that time. From this we take out the place of the ascendant in the zodiac under the Tables of Oblique Ascension or Tables of Houses, and thus get the directional ascendant. Similarly the arc of direction is added to the longitude of the Sun, also to that of the Moon and that of Fortuna.

Thus we have the five significators all directed in the zodiac by an arc of mean longitude equivalent to the age of the person. Taking each of these in turn, we note the aspects that they form when thus placed, and these constitute the direct directions of the significators.

Next, we add the same arc of direction to the longitudes of Neptune, Uranus, Saturn, Jupiter, Mars, Venus, and Mercury, and from these directional places we note what aspects they form to the radical places of the five significators. This completes the entire series of current primary directions.

SECONDARY DIRECTIONS.—The mean increment of the Sun's longitude having been used for the calculation of primary indications, we must similarly use that of the Moon for the calculation of secondaries, for the geocentric periods of the Sun and Moon bear a definite relation to one another. The mean acceleration of the Moon may be taken as 13° 10′ per day, and just as the Sun's mean increment of 59′ 8″ is taken for the annual direction at the rate of one day for a year, so that annual direction of the Moon will be 13° 10′. This gives a mensual increment of 1° 6′ nearly, which may be adjusted by making the increment 1° 5′ only every sixth month.

For the purpose of immediately applying these increments of the Sun and Moon to the radical longitudes in order to get the directional longitudes for any given age of a person, see the Tables of Mean Motion given in Appendix A, pp. 159, 160.

The following example will make the method of

direction and the use of the tables quite clear to the student:

HOROSCOPE OF DAVID LLOYD GEORGE, PRIME MINISTER.
Liverpool, January 17, 1863, at 8h. 57m. a.m.

♌ 14	♐ 27	♐ 9° 56′	♏ 19	♎ 15
26° ☉ 49′ ♀ 5° 46′ ♏ 10° 22	⊕ 8° 7′	☽ 24° 33′	♃ 26° 25′	♄ 5° 22′ ♒ 10° 22′ ♌
☿ 12° 19′ ♓ 1° ♆ 27′	1° ♂ 2′		♅ 17° 18′	
♈ 15	♉ 19	♊ 9° 56′	♊ 27	♋ 14

Example.—The Right Hon. David Lloyd George, Prime Minister of H.M. Government, born at Liverpool, January 17, 1863, at 8.57 a.m. In January, 1917, the "little Welshman," as he is fondly called by his admirers, though he is not little in stature and is great in many other respects, reached his fifty-fourth birthday anniversary. The arc for this age is 53° 14′. Adding this to the place of the significators in the radical horoscope, a copy of which is here reproduced, we have the following positions of direction:

Mid-heaven	..	.. Aquarius 3° 10′
Ascendant	..	.. Gemini 10° 3′
Sun	..	.. Pisces 20° 3′
Moon	..	.. Aquarius 17° 43′
Fortuna	..	.. Pisces 1° 21′

These places are directed to the radical mid-heaven, ascendant, Sun, Moon, and planets. By observation we get the following indications:

THE RADIX SYSTEM

Mid-heaven *ab* square Mars, sextile Neptune, sesquare Uranus, *ad* trine Saturn, trine Venus.
Ascendant opposition mid-heaven, *ad* trine Mercury.
Sun *ab* square Uranus, *ad* semisquare Venus, square Moon, semisquare Fortuna.
Moon trine Uranus.
Fortuna sextile Mars.

We now have to deal with the directional places of the planets. They are found by adding the same arc of direction to their radical longitudes, and the aspects formed to the significators may be noted:

Neptune .. Taurus 24° 41' *ad* trine Sun.
Uranus .. Leo 10° 32' opposition ascendant, *ab* sesquare Moon.
Saturn .. Scorpio 28° 36' *ab* sextile Sun.
Jupiter .. Sagittarius 19° 39', no aspect to significators.
Mars .. Gemini 24° 16', opposition Moon.
Venus .. Pisces 29° 1', *ab* sextile Sun.
Mercury .. Aries 5° 33', *ad* square Fortuna.

Collating these, we find the following in operation at the time of the *coup d'état* by which the Rump Parliament of Asquith was suddenly brought to an end by the formation of the new War Ministry under Lloyd George, and the concurrent attempt upon the life of the Premier by poisoning:

PRIMARY DIRECTIONS (1917).

Mid-heaven ad trine Saturn, trine Venus.
Ascendant opposition mid-heaven.
Sun semisquare Venus.
Moon trine Uranus.
Fortuna sextile Mars.
Uranus opposition ascendant.
Mars opposition Moon.

These directions are extremely significant. The opposition of the ascendant to the mid-heaven set Lloyd George, then Minister of Munitions, against the Government and his superior in office, whose "Wait and See" policy was threatening the most vital interests of the country and causing the gravest discontent throughout the Empire. The success which attended the efforts of Lloyd George at the time when he was called upon by the King to form a Cabinet and save the country from its peril is well indicated by the directions:

> Moon trine Uranus,
> Fortuna sextile Mars,

which gave him that degree of democratic support necessary to effectively uphold the majority of public opinion, and stimulated him to a truly remarkable display of energy and whole-hearted efficiency in the great task which fell to his lot.

But the danger which threatened, and of which he was duly warned through a reputable intermediary conversant with the facts of astrology, was all too apparent to me, for the Moon (hyleg) was afflicted by the opposition of Mars from the sign Gemini, and the ascendant by the opposition of Uranus from the sign Leo.

The transits of the major planets at this time (December, 1916) show Neptune opposition midheaven, and Uranus exactly opposition Moon's directional place. But when in August, 1917, and during the month of September, the planet Jupiter came to the directional ascendant, and was stationary there, the administration was seen to bear the very best results, and matters connected with munitions, equipment, provender, transport, and foreign relations were such as to cause the greatest satisfaction throughout the country; and astrologers looked forward to April, 1918, with the greatest confidence, for then the same planet transits the ascendant of this directional horoscope. It was this position of Jupiter which set off the opposition of Mars and Saturn to the ascendant of the radical horoscope in October, 1917, but it did not prevent something in the nature of a crisis over the proposed Swedish-German Convention at Stockholm, and the consequent resignation of Mr. Henderson from the Ministry and the repudiation of Ramsay Macdonald

THE RADIX SYSTEM

by the electorate of Leicester, represented by him in Parliament.

We may now turn to the secondary directions at the fifty-fourth anniversary, and show how they are calculated and judged:

To the radical place of the Moon in longitude		8ˢ 24° 33'
Add for fifty-four years		11ˢ 21° 32'
		8ˢ 16° 5'

Which gives the Moon's place by mean motion in Sagittarius 16° 5' on January 17, 1917, from which subtract seventeen days' motion 37', and we get the longitude for January 1 in Sagittarius 15° 28'. We then successively add for the first of each succeeding month 1° 6', and obtain the following scale of directions to the radical and directional places of the significators and planets:

SECONDARIES (1917).

January	..	15 ♐	28
February	..	16	34 ☍ ♅ □⁴
March	..	17	40 ∠ M C ♒¹⁰, ⚹ ☽ ♒¹
April	..	18	46
May	..	19	52 ∠ ♀ ♒¹², □ ☉ ⚹¹, ☌ ♃¹⁰
June*	..	20	57
July	..	22	3
August	..	23	9
September	..	24	15 ☌ ☽ ♐¹¹, ☍ ☌ □⁵
October	..	25	21 ⚹ ♃ ♎⁸, Q ♄ ♐⁷
November	..	26	27 ∠ ♀ ♒¹
December*	..	27	32

Explanation.—In reviewing these indications we must not leave out of sight the fact that they are entirely subsidiary to the primaries in force, and that in order to form primary directions the planets have

* These two months are equated—1' to adjust to the mean annual motion. The figures following the signs indicate the house from which the planets operate in either the radix or directional horoscope.

to be carried forward in the zodiac at the rate of nearly 1 degree per year. Thus, in order to form the primary indication Uranus opposition ascendant, we have to advance Uranus to the 11th degree of Leo; and when, therefore, in October, 1917, the Moon comes by secondary mean motion to the sesquare of Uranus, the influence of the planet is exerted, not as in February, from the fourth house, but from the seventh house. Similarly, Jupiter by direction has reached Sagittarius 20°, and is therefore in the radical tenth house, the Moon coming to the conjunction in May, 1917. The influences have to be interpreted in terms of the radix, so far as the house position is concerned, for although the planets are directed to change of sign, and the signs themselves pass by direction into different houses, yet the houses themselves remain fixed and unalterable in their position and significance. That is why the coming of Jupiter to the tenth house by direction coincided with the powerful campaign which gave to Lloyd George his immense democratic representation in Parliament, which finally led to the curtailment of the powers of the House of Lords.

Summary.—In effect, therefore, we have here presented a system of directing which maintains the mutual relations of the planets in the radix, and which preserves the interpretation of directional indications in terms of the radix, while at the same time the greatest simplicity of calculation is secured by the conversion of arcs into mean increment of longitude, and finally proves itself in practice to be altogether reliable as a means of prognosis. More than this cannot be expected of any system, and very much less has for some centuries satisfied the laborious and patient student.

HOROSCOPICAL ANOMALIES.

STUDENTS of the law of sex and the prenatal epoch as defined by me in the "Manual of Astrology," and since elaborated in association with the researches of Mr. E. H. Bailey, will be interested in the following study. It is a case of biovate twins born in the northwest of England at the following times: October 31, 1873, first at 5.40 p.m., second at 5.50 p.m., both Greenwich mean time. I may explain that biovate twins are such as are born from two distinct amnions as the result of the impregnation of two separate ova, as distinguished from monovate twins born from a double impregnation of one and the same ovum. My readers will find some most interesting information on this subject in Sir Francis Galton's "Inquiries into Human Faculty."

Taking the two births as recorded, and applying the prenatal epoch rules to them, the first-born comes out at 5h. 38m. 28s. p.m., and the second comes out at 5h. 51m. 58s. p.m., G.M.T. The first-born was practically an eight-months' child, and the second-born was a full nine-months' child, the epoch of the first being March 5, 1873, at 6h. 52m. 11s., G.M.T, and the second being February 6, at 8h. 38m. 46s., G.M.T. Computed from the original time of birth in each case, the epoch affords the following comparisons:

1. *Birth.*—Asc. ♊ 5° 46' | October 31, 1873.
       Moon ♓ 14° 40' | 5h. 38m. 58s. p.m.

  Epoch.—Moon ♊ 5° 46' | March 5, 1873.
       Asc. ♈ 14° 40' | 6h. 52m. 11s. a.m.

2.—*Birth.*—Asc. ♊ 10° 21' | October 31, 1873.
        Moon ♓ 14° 46' | 5h. 51m. 58s. p.m.

Epoch.—Moon ♊ 10° 21' | February 6, 1873.
        Asc. ♓ 14° 46' | 8h. 38m. 46s. a.m.

Now I must state a few remarkable facts in connection with these two natives. The first-born (the last conceived) became engaged in the fall of 1897, was married in February, 1899, was taken ill on March 1, 1899, and died on March 11, 1899. The second-born (first conceived) is unmarried at the date of writing, and is in normal good health.

Now I will ask any intelligent student of astrology to erect the two horoscopes of these nativities, one for 5.40 p.m., and the other for 5.50 p.m., and see if something is not wanting to distinguish between the fortunes of one and the other of these natives.

The prenatal epoch solves the difficult problem It presumes as a basis of its rationale that at back of the personality there is an individual pressing forward towards expression, that the horoscope of birth represents merely the environment of the individual—the conditions, in fact, through which the individual has to function—while the epoch horoscope represents, in a more intimate manner, the nature of the individual itself as divested of the conditions of sex, heredity, etc., imported into the birth by means of the body it is clothed with. Hence in the above remarkable case we have two distinct individuals, the ratio of force in each being different and distinct, the innate tendencies divergent, yet both called upon to find expression through what is practically the same environment, horoscopically and socially.

Let us see how these statements are borne out in the two cases before us. Referring to the epoch for the first-born, March 5, 1873, at 6.52 p.m., we find Pisces 14° 40' rising with the Moon in the sign Gemini 5° 45' on the cusp of the third house, in zodiacal square aspect to the Sun, which is exactly rising and in mundane square to both Saturn and Uranus. The Sun has the semisquare aspect of Saturn, and Jupiter is in the sixth house and Mars in the eighth, both being rulers of the ascendant.

Take the second on February 6, 1873, at 8.39 p.m., and we find Pisces 14° 46' rising with the Moon advanced into the third house, and going to the trine of the Sun in Aquarius.

In the first case the Moon is square to the Sun, while in the second case it is trine to the Sun. The horoscopes, in fact, are very different at the two epochs.

The student will at once perceive that, on account of the short interval of time between the two births, the radical horoscopes are practically identical, and the directions (diurnal) of the one and the other would coincide to within three days of any given event. Hence it is not in that direction that we must look for light upon the divergence of destiny in the two cases. We must again consult the directions from the two epochs, and we shall find them as dissimilar as the two lives have been. It is to be noted how dangerous it is even for an experienced astrologer to maintain, without full possession of the facts of the subject under debate, such a doctrine as the following: "The natal hour is far the most important epoch of any."

Taking the epoch, March 5, 1873, at 6.52 a.m., and calculating to the time of the death, it will be found that Mars comes out of the eighth house into opposition with the ascendant, while the Moon forms the mundane opposition of the meridian and the mundane square of the ascendant, while the Sun forms the mundane square of the Moon. By secondary or diurnal motion the Moon has reached the longitude Taurus 24° 16', where it forms the square aspect of Jupiter in the sixth house.

Now turn to the nativity, October 31, 1873, at 5.38 p.m., and it will be seen that at the rate of a day for a year the Moon has reached Aquarius, 17° 19' with declin. 20° 6' at the time of the illness, which proved fatal in ten days. It forms no aspects, but the Sun has the parallel of Saturn. If we compare the directions from the nativity with the radical positions at the epoch, we shall find that the Sun is approaching the opposition of the Moon in the epoch, and hence by inference the opposition of the ascendant of the natal horoscope. At the same time it will be observed that the Sun by direction from the epoch has just reached the opposition of Venus in the nativity on the cusp of the sixth house.

To sum up the matter, it appears most conspicuously that the natal horoscope is *not* the most important epoch of any, for, if it were so, then it would have to be shown why, in these two horoscopes, which are so nearly related as to be practically identical for all judicial purposes, the Sun parallel Saturn should kill in the one case and not in the other. There must have been a mortal predisposition in the case of the first-born of the twins, and this we see to have been the case. The cause of death is stated to have been appendicitis, ending with one day's illness from peritonitis.

For further evidence of the paramount value of the prenatal lunar epoch in the determination of individual fortunes and anomalies arising out of twin births, both monovate and biovate, the reader is referred to "The Prenatal Epoch," by E. H. Bailey.*

---

* London: W. Foulsham and Co., Ltd., 61, Fleet Street, E.C

STUDIES IN BRIEF

1. FEMALE, born in London, May 2, 1891. The Sun applies to the square aspect of Uranus, retrograde in the sign Aquarius, then to square of Saturn. She was married for three years; her husband deserted her. The Sun forms the square of Uranus three days after birth. Seventeen days later ♅ turns direct, and the husband returns.

Axiom.—When the ☉ in a female horoscope applies to an evil aspect of ♅, separation or desertion will ensue.

2. Male child, born near London, March 11, 1897, at 5 p.m. Burned to death while playing with matches on June 15, 1899.

The student will, on reference to the ephemeris, at once seize upon the chief significators of this fatality. The Moon is found in the tenth house in the sign ♊, and in close conjunction with Mars and Neptune, the satellite being in square aspect to the Sun in the seventh house. It will be observed that on the day of the accident the Moon was transiting the ascendant of the horoscope, while the Sun, Mercury and Neptune were conjoined in close proximity to Mars, Moon, and Mercury therein, Saturn being in opposition. The solar eclipse of June 8 immediately preceding fell within 3° of the place of the ☉ (hyleg).

Axiom.—The Moon in ♊, in conjunction with Mars and Neptune, threatens death by fire, and it is the more certain if at the same time the Sun be similarly afflicted.

3. Lady, born February 14, 1853, 4.10 a.m., London.

Married and lost her husband in fifteen months. Sagittarius rises with ♃ therein. The Sun falls in the second house in conjunction with Mars. Venus has the square aspect of Uranus and the Moon, the latter being in conjunction with Uranus. The Sun first forms the sextile of Uranus.

Axiom.—When Venus is afflicted by an evil aspect of Uranus or Saturn, domestic troubles ensue. When the Sun is afflicted by Mars in a female geniture, the husband is in danger of an early death.

4. Male, born in London, April 9, 1862, at 1.41 p.m. M.C. right ascension = 42° 49'. Lost his mother March, 1891, and his father June, 1891. The *primary directions* for these events are Asc. ☌ ♄ zod. d. 28° 53', M.C. ☌ ♅ m. d. 29° 10.' The Moon by *secondary direction* was in conjunction with Saturn and Jupiter at the father's death, and in square to Uranus at the mother's death. Saturn, Jupiter, and the Moon were exactly on the progressed ascendant at the father's death, and the event brought a legacy. Three months earlier the Moon square ♅ on the mid-heaven of the directional horoscope indicated the death of the mother.

Axiom.—When Saturn and Jupiter conspire to the production of an event, there is generally a silver lining to the cloud. The mid-heaven and ascendant have some relation to the family fortunes, as indicating the parents and their estate. The ascendant is directed by oblique ascension in the zodiac, and the mid-heaven by right ascension in the zodiac.

5. E. R. B., female, born September 9, 1856, at 11.7 a.m., in Madras, India. The right ascension of M.C. = 155° 8' = ♍ 3° 7'. The ascendant is ♐ 2° 9'. The ☉ in the tenth house first applies to ☍ ♆ R. Her married life was marred by the defection and chaotic habits of her husband, who died before her, leaving a family of two boys. The ☽ is in the second house in ♑, and opposed by ♄ in ♋ from the eighth house. The lady was passionately fond of flowers (♀ in ♎), and it was while gathering them from the hills that she

fell and sustained a severe contusion which developed into uterine cancer. She died on May 26, 1899, at 5 p.m. (Madras time), after three months of intense suffering, her age at the time of the event being 42 y. 8 m. 17 d.=42° 42' of right ascension. The right ascension of ♄ is 103° 17', its meridian distance being 51° 51', and its semi-arc 94° 33'. The arc of direction of *Saturn to the opposition of the ascendant* is therefore 42° 42', Saturn being in the eighth house at birth in the sign ♋ (Cancer).

The student will notice the point of fatality, calculated from ♄ in the eighth, falls on the place of Venus. The lady was an extremely good horsewoman until she met with an injury indicated by ♅ in the sixth, ☍ ♂ in twelfth, from ♉ and ♏. The artistic sense was well developed, and found expression in a variety of ways. Her nature was gentle and refined, but fearless, proud, and independent. An indulgent enemy, a staunch friend, very much beloved by many of her own sex, and favoured with the confidence of both men and women. Her aged parents survived her. The *secondary directions* were very insignificant, though the ☽ was separating from par. ♄ P. and applying to par. ♂ R.

Axiom.—The direction of a planet from the eighth house to the opposition of the ascendant generally proves a dangerous if not fatal period, and this is more to be feared if the planet thus directed be at birth badly situated and in evil aspect to other bodies.

OUR SOLAR SYSTEM.

Some following brief notes, in addition to those given in my 'Astrologer's Ready Reckoner,' may prove very helpful to many readers in their efforts to comprehend the magnitude and operations of the solar system. The mass of the Sun is 332,260 times greater than the Earth, and about 749 times greater than all the planets put together. The diameter of the Sun, according to the latest measurements, is 866,200 miles, giving a surface of 2,357,127,702,000 square miles, and the enormous volume of 340,289,375,000,000 cubic miles. By keeping these figures in sight you will appreciate the fact that our Sun is truly king of the solar system as we proceed to give similar figures concerning each of the principal planets.

Mercury at greatest distance from the Sun is 43,347,000, at least distance 28,569,000, and at average distance 35,958,000 miles away from the great central orb—nearly twice as far away as at perihelion. He travels around the Sun in eighty-eight of our days. His greatest distance from Earth is 137,797,000 miles, least distance 47,983,000 miles. He is the most dense of planets. His actual diameter is 3,008 miles, giving 28,431,000 square and 14,255,000,000 cubic miles of surface and volume. He rotates on his axis in 24h., 5m. 30s., turning 392 miles an hour at his equator. His average orbital velocity is 107,012 miles per hour.

Venus, second planet, is, when at greatest distance, 67,652,000 miles from Sun, and 66,728,000 miles when nearest, showing the Sun is much nearer the centre of

OUR SOLAR SYSTEM

her orbit than Mercury's. She goes round the Sun in 224 days and a fraction, rotates on her axis in 23h. 21m. 23s., moving at equator 1,006 miles per hour. Her orbital velocity is 78,284 miles per hour. Her diameter is 7,480 miles, giving her 175,783,000 square miles of surface and a volume of 219,149,000,000 cubic miles. Greatest distance from Earth 162,102,000 miles, least distance 23,678,000. This accounts for the vast difference in her apparent size. When her diameter seems smallest she is more nearly round, the sunlight on more of her surface being reflected to us. Venus is the nearest planet to Earth.

Earth's greatest distance from the Sun is 94,450,000 miles, and least distance 91,330,000 miles. It is 7,926 miles in diameter, having a surface of 197,309,000 square miles and a volume of 260,613,000,000 cubic miles. It rotates on its axis in 23h. 56m. 4s., travelling in its orbit 66,570 miles per hour, its rotary speed at equator being 1,040 miles per hour. Our year is 365.256 days. In many respects as much is known of the other planets as of the Earth.

War-god Mars varies in distance from the Sun from 128,358,000 miles at nearest to 154,714,000 miles at greatest. His time of revolution around the Sun is about 587 days; rotates on his axis in 24h. 37m. 23s. He moves in his orbit 53,938 miles per hour, turning 638 miles per hour on his equator. Is 4,999 miles in diameter, containing 78,503,000 surface square and 65,403,000,000 cubic miles. Greatest distance from Earth 248,164,000 and least 33,908,000 miles.

Jupiter is greater than all planets in the solar system put together. Greatest distance from Sun 506,563,000 miles, least 460,013,000 miles. He goes around the Sun in about 4,332 days, travels in his orbit 29,203 miles per hour, and rotates at his equator 28,001 miles per hour, making a complete rotation on his axis in 9h. 55m. 21s. Greatest distance from Earth 601,013,000 miles, least 365,563,000 miles. Is 88,439 miles in diameter, having 24,571,480,000

150 THE SCIENCE OF FOREKNOWLEDGE

square surface miles and 362,178,000,000,000 cubic miles.

Saturn, with his rings and moons, is the greatest wonder of the solar system. No sane mind can ever forget the impressions made by a good telescopic view of this planet. His maximum distance from Sun is 931.033,000 miles, minimum 841,097,000. He revolves around the Sun in 10,759 days. Orbital velocity 21,560 miles per hour. Speed of rotation at equator, 22,476 miles per hour, requiring only 10h. 29m. 17s. for a complete rotation of its axis. Diameter of planet, 75,036 miles, giving him a surface of 17,688,537,000 square miles and a volume of 221,217,083,000,000 cubic miles. The open circular space between planet and first ring is 18,640 miles across, the ring itself being 16,765 miles broad. The interval of space between the two rings is 1,750 miles, being so small that a good telescope is required to separate them. The outer ring is 10,320 miles broad, giving a complete diameter of the planet and rings of 172,240 miles. Saturn has eight moons, some of which are visible in small telescopes.

Samuel Elliott Coves developed and published in his work on "The Earth" in 1860 the astronomical constant 109·62, which is of great use in solving intricate astronomical problems. Thus, if we multiply the diameter of the Moon, 2,160 miles by 109·62, we have its mean distance from the Earth=236,779 miles. The diameter of the Sun, 852,584 miles × 109·32=94,460,258 miles, its near distance. The constant 109·62 has an interesting genesis. The periodic time of the Earth is 365·24 days. This number multiplied by π or 3·1416=1,147·437984, the square of which is 1,316,700, the cube root of which is 109·62. The distance of the Earth from the Sun divided by the diameter of the Sun=109·62, which is therefore the Sun diameters contained in the assumed distance.

It may be a little disconcerting to the advanced Western intellect to learn that this very number was used as a constant for the number of days (reduced to the lowest terms) in which the Sun, Moon, and planets would simultaneously complete their revolutions and come to the same position in the heavens—in other words, it represents the Kalpa. The number is used by the Hindus in computing the mean longitudes of the planets for any period of time as set forth in the "Suryasiddhanta" and other Indian works of antiquity.

FINANCIAL ASTROLOGY

THERE is a philosophy that begins and ends in the skies, immeasurably above the heads of the Earth-born sons of toil, remote from the daily life of man, hidden from his apprehension by the great void of insensible space, bounded on the higher and farther side by the unearthly and on the nether and nigher by the unpractical. This is the astrology (falsely called " practical ") that exhausts itself in myth and symbol, like fragments taken from a coloured oriel and set in a kaleidoscope for the entertainment of a wonder-loving, speculative imagination. Its advocates have, doubtless, very definite views as to the advantages they derive from its study. To them it is a religion, a star-lit pathway winding upward to Parnassus. But, like all true religion, the wonder and the joy of it are incommunicable.

To thresh out the colours of the rainbow on a granite rock may be fit sport for the gods, but we of the Earth are quite content to see them swimming in a barrel of tar. We disentangle the rainbow from the black mass, and find that we still have left a thousand beautiful perfumes and still more useful things; but the rain-drops dry off the granite, the sun sets, and the cold, grey glint of the rock is all that is left of the rainbow. All nature is on the side of the practical and the useful. Let our astrologers seek, therefore, to be practical.

Many years ago it was said to us: " Make your astrology practical, and the world will follow you." The man who voiced this remark was already convinced of its truth: he only failed to see its practical value. This, in brief, is our object—to demonstrate the practical value of astrology. We have to bring the stars down to Earth, to interpret them into the language of everyday life; in short, to give the man in the street a science of foreknowledge he can turn to his advantage. For some years past we have studied astrology in relation to the world's commercial and financial interests, and have brought the light of the stars to bear upon the dark problem of future values. We are now in a position to controvert all the pet maxims of the market, to effectively skin " bear " and " bull," and show them in all their nakedness to the world as of the same flesh and blood—*the unconscious interpreters of planetary influence*. We can make capital out of any and every transaction in which the " time " element is optional.

How can we do this? By a knowledge of the law of periodicity as revealed in our method of financial astrology. We know it can be done, for we have stood the test—not once, but often. Possibly we do not come up to the idea of the traditional star-gazer. The fire of prophecy that burns in the eye and wastes the flesh in nightly vigils and austerities, the skull-cap and spectacles, and the out-of-date dressing-gown scribbled o'er with the mystical symbols of the heavens, find no place in the paraphernalia of our art. There is never even the ghost of a black cat perched upon our shoulders. But what we lack in the externals of the craft we can make good by a closer contact with the ordinary wayfarer and a finer sympathy with his nature and his needs, for they are similar to our own in every way. The level Earth is good enough for the man with a good ambition; he has no need of a platform or a pedestal. He can touch the crowd if he knows its needs; he can move the world if he can move himself.

Astrology is not a religion. It will never save a soul from self-destruction; but as a science it will throw light—a welcome light—upon the dark and narrow paths through which a hungry and belated soul may have to force its way. Where there was tyranny and servitude, oppression and slavery, opulence and indigence, happiness and misery, and an infinity of chance conditions in a world already made, the light will reveal a universal service of infinite opportunity occurring to each and every soul in a world that is for ever in the making, for the teachings of astrology are practical.

All trade and commerce is of the nature of a speculative investment or enterprise. Because a man is finite and has a limited knowledge of the conditions that prevail at any given moment, and a still more limited knowledge of the conditions that will thereafter obtain, every act comes to be of the nature of a speculation. We point this fact because there are those good people, well-meaning, but deplorably short-sighted, who cannot conceive of capital apart from labour, forgetting that a good constitution, a well-balanced brain, a special faculty, and an opportunity to use these, are *capital* that the individual has not earned by any labour of his own. They forget that capital is not always expressed in gold, but that more often it is the means of purchasing gold. While all that the Earth produces apart from human labour is a free gift to man, we may safely drop the discussion of *meum* and *tuum*, and lay our hands upon all we can utilize.

Who are " the horny-handed sons of toil " that they should be preferred to the artist, musician, or poet? They produce nothing; they only develop that which Nature has produced, or so much of it as fortune and capital have placed within reach. The tiller of the soil, the working farmer, whose occupation is universally regarded as the most simple and honest, delves in that which he did not produce, and lives in hope that the seed he has sown will yield in its season. He invests labour, but he speculates heavily in earthquakes and lightning! The tradesman who gets in a stock of comestibles, and fills his store with them, undertakes a liability which he hopes to meet by selling them at a profit. He does not buy to order only. He, too, speculates. In short, those who require to call speculation by another name before they can call it honest ought to beware how they eat their daily bread. It would be better did they " consider the lilies !"

If astrology is to be of any use to mankind, it must eventually touch the " bread-and-butter " considerations of the million. Nay, more; it must be made to translate bread and butter into cake and cream. Not till then will its more sublime aspects claim the attention of the world. People will be more disposed to submit themselves to the laws of Heaven when life on Earth is made more pleasant for them. The fact may be an occasion for self-reproach, but it is yet a fact, and has to be reckoned with. The old Adam is a strong gaoler —a terrible brute of a fellow. Get him to sleep, put him at his ease, give him plenty to eat and drink, and something not so hard as stone to lie upon, and we are free to disport ourselves as we list. Those who have wings can use them.

So that even the gospel of the millennium, which promises a competence to every man and a universal peace, begins and ends with the things of this world, and brings us no nigher Heaven than Earth itself can be lifted.

The line of least resistance is that of greatest progress. To work along with the forces of Nature, to keep to the old and well-worn grooves, and follow the courses of the stars—this is the secret of success in life. Put aside your own judgment, which you have proved thousands of times to be fallible, and *follow the law*.

Why did Joseph Leiter fail to work his corner in wheat? It was elaborately engineered, and as fine a piece of commercial generalship as anything of the kind on record—save that of his namesake in Egypt, in the days of the Pharaoh, Ramses. Joseph Leiter was backed by the kings of commerce, and had the market practically in his hands. Then why did he fail? Simply because *he got out of gear with the machinery of the heavens* at a certain stage of the running. The exact date was May 6, 1898, when the market was forced up against the downward impulse of celestial energy. He upheld the market for four days, and then became aware that he had driven prices too high, and that the only thing to be done was to let them down again as gently as he could. How do we know this? By practical commercial astrology. Did we not predict the big rise in August, 1897, in *Coming Events;* that of October, 1897 (*ibid.*, ii., pp. 18, 19); the slump of mid-November, 1897 (*ibid.*, p. 78); the rise in January, 1898 (*ibid.*, p. 142); that of February, 1898, (*ibid.*, p. 199); the great boom in April (*ibid.*, p.p. 214 and 268); the depression in August (*ibid.*, p. 487); and the rise in September, as well as the chief movements in the stock markets from month to month and from week to week? Correspondents (whose letters are open to inspection) have written in the pages of *Coming Events*, showing that we not only had foreknowledge of these movements, but also their extent; and when we saw that Mr. Leiter had made a wrong move we wrote to some of our clients, so that they might not be carried off their feet by the reaction.

Mr. Leiter erred doubly. He overstocked himself, and he drove up prices too high. With a smaller corner at less ambitious prices he could have come out the gainer by half a million dollars between April 10 and May 6. He lifted prices up to April 23, lowered them to the 30th, lifted again to May 5. So far he was *in harmony with the law*. But when he further inflated the market, from the 6th to the 10th, instead of clearing out and letting it go down, he committed an error that, in one so ambitious and so well equipped, might almost be called a sin. He resisted the law, and came under its lash.

Action and reaction are equal and opposite. Everything in Nature tends towards an equilibrium. Life and operation are continually disturbing that equilibrium. The normal level of things (parity) is constantly being touched. The man who would deal with the abnormal must first study the normal. A stock rises, being at the time above par. Hundreds of "bulls" rush in to take the profit, knowing (or perhaps not knowing), as they ought, that the trend of that stock is naturally towards parity, and not knowing how far the passing impulse will take it. Here is the secret of our knowledge!

The passing rise is only a preliminary of a heavy fall to something below par. When a quickly moving vessel is put hard a-port, it moves to starboard before answering to its rudder. The circumstance has deceived thousands of those who have newly embarked on the ship of commerce. To traffic in strange waters one must know the running currents as well as the ebb and flow of the tides. *Astrology supplies this information.*

What would be the effect of this knowledge becoming universal? Would not all operators on the market become "bulls" or "bears" simultaneously? Certainly not. There must be something to trade before you can buy it. You cannot buy what does not exist, even though you may sell what you have not got—but what, nevertheless, you undertake to acquire. "Bulls" would buy at lowest, "bears" would sell at highest. The "bulls" would inflate the market for the ultimate benefit of the "bears," the latter would deflate it for the benefit of prospective "bulls." "Bull" and "bear" are mere hides. You may find the same creature wearing both.

If astrology were to become as popular as its advantages are great, the result would be that fluctuations would be more intense, higher and lower, on either side of the normal. *The periodicity would remain as it is—a reflex of astral impulse.*

Here is the great key to success! We can tell you when any stock or produce will turn, when it will be lowest, when highest, when to buy, when to sell—

cutting both ways, buying at lowest for the rise, and selling at highest for the fall.

This is practical astrology. But it is not all astrology is capable of, it is not by any means the highest or best that it can afford; but it is what the world wants of it by way of passport to higher honours—and the world can have it for the asking.

Those of my readers who wish to pursue the study of financial astrology further are recommended to read my "Law of Values," which I claim to be the soundest instruction that prospective investors have ever had placed before them. Those, on the other hand, who are disposed to bank upon "outside" chances and to speculate in accordance with the law of celestial influence will find my "Arcana" to be their safest guide. They include keys to the stock and share markets, the various produce markets—*e.g.*, wheat, cotton, sugar, wool, etc.—and keys to sporting speculation of all kinds. They prove beyond all doubt the existence of a well-defined law where hitherto we have spoken only of "chance" and "luck." In the midst of so many dreamers it is well for one astrologer to be practical.

APPENDIX

TO FIND SIDEREAL TIME AND SIGN ON MID-HEAVEN AT ANY HOUR.

Table I.

Month.	Constant.	Month.	Constant
	h. m.		h. m.
January	18 35	July	6 30
February	20 38	August	8 32
March	22 30	September	10 34
April	0 31	October	12 32
May	2 30	November	14 34
June	4 32	December	16 33

EXAMPLE.—What was the approximate sidereal time at 2h. 30m. p.m. on January 15, 1876?

	h.	m.
Date or month, 15 × 4' = 60', or	1	0
Constant for the month of January	18	35
Time elapsed since last noon	2	30
Sidereal time required	22	5

N.B.—Had the time been 2h. 30m. a.m. we would have added 14h. 30m., the time elapsed since last noon. When the sidereal time exceeds 24 hours use the excess of 24 hours.

Table II.

Sidereal Time.	Sign Transiting the M.C.	Sidereal Time.	Sign Transiting the M.C.
h. m.		h. m.	
0 0	Aries.	13 51	Libra.
1 51	Aries.	13 52	Scorpio.
1 52	Taurus.	15 51	Scorpio.
3 51	Taurus.	15 52	Sagittarius.
3 52	Gemini.	17 59	Sagittarius.
5 59	Gemini.	18 0	Capricornus.
6 0	Cancer.	20 8	Capricornus.
8 8	Cancer.	20 9	Aquarius.
8 9	Leo.	22 8	Aquarius.
10 8	Leo.	22 9	Pisces.
10 9	Virgo.	23 59	Pisces.
11 59	Virgo.	24 0	Aries.
12 0	Libra.	1 51	Aries.

Table III.—Primary and Secondary Arcs.

Years.				Months.			
Primary.		Secondary.		Primary.		Secondary.	
	Deg. Min.	s Deg. Min.			Min.	Deg. Min.	
1 ...	0 59	0 13 11		1 ...	5	1 6	
2 ...	1 58	0 26 21		2 ...	10	2 12	
3 ...	2 57	1 9 32		3 ...	15	3 18	
4 ...	3 57	1 22 42		4 ...	20	4 24	
5 ...	4 56	2 5 53		5 ...	25	5 29	
6 ...	5 55	2 19 3		6 ...	30	6 35	
7 ...	6 54	3 2 14		7 ...	35	7 41	
8 ...	7 53	3 15 25		8 ...	39	8 47	
9 ...	8 52	3 28 35		9 ...	44	9 53	
10 ...	9 51	4 11 46		10 ...	49	10 59	
20 ...	19 43	8 23 32		11 ...	54	12 5	
30 ...	29 34	1 5 18		12 ...	59	13 11	
40 ...	39 26	5 17 4					
50 ...	49 17	9 28 50					
60 ...	59 8	2 10 36					